Let Us Begin

Let Us Begin

Saint Francis's Way of Becoming Like Christ and Renewing the World

Thomas Griffin

Foreword by Fr. Mark-Mary Ames, CFR

Our Sunday Visitor
Huntington, Indiana

Nihil Obstat
Msgr. Michael Heintz, Ph.D.
Censor Librorum

Imprimatur
✠ Kevin C. Rhoades
Bishop of Fort Wayne-South Bend
May 3, 2024

The *Nihil Obstat* and *Imprimatur* are official declarations that a book is free from doctrinal or moral error. It is not implied that those who have granted the *Nihil Obstat* and *Imprimatur* agree with the contents, opinions, or statements expressed.

Our Sunday Visitor Publishing Division
Our Sunday Visitor, Inc.
200 Noll Plaza
Huntington, IN 46750
www.osv.com
1-800-348-2440

ISBN: 978-1-63966-070-4 (Inventory No. T2811)
1. RELIGION—Christianity—Saints & Sainthood.
2. RELIGION—Christian Living—Spiritual Growth.
3. RELIGION—Christianity—Catholic.
eISBN: 978-1-63966-071-1
LCCN: 2024940614

Cover design: Tyler Ottinger
Interior design: Amanda Falk
Cover art: AdobeStock

Printed in the United States of America

Because of Joanna

Contents

Contents

Foreword

Fr. Mark-Mary Ames, CFR

The mere mention of her name changed the trajectory of my life. I was eighteen years old and helping out with a youth retreat at Big Bear Mountain in Orange County, California. A speaker had been brought in to preach to the teenagers preparing for their confirmation. In the midst of his roughly twenty-minute talk, about one minute was used on some passing comments about Mother Teresa. It was a minute that would change me.

I don't remember the gist of the talk, and it certainly wasn't a talk on Mother Teresa, but in a few passing comments he mentioned Mother Teresa and the work she had been doing in Calcutta before her death. For the Holy Spirit, this was enough to work with. In an instant, a truth that the Divine Author had written on my heart from the very beginning of my life became legible for the first time: I was made to give my life to the poorest of the poor, and nothing else would satisfy. Immediately my heart began to burn with a fire that burns to this day: "I want to live and love and be poured out like Mother Teresa. That alone will satisfy the deepest desires of my heart."

I didn't meet Mother Teresa. She didn't sit me down and give me some pastoral counseling and guidance. I didn't read any of her works, nor did I watch a documentary about her life. She wasn't even alive when all of this happened. Yet she was the vessel of grace that the Lord used to awaken my heart and draw me to him in the Eucharist and the poor. This is the power of holiness. This is the power of the saints. Saints and sanctity are always the answer.

At this point, the reader may find it a little bit curious why a book on Saint Francis is begun with a story about Mother Teresa. The Franciscan Friars of the Renewal, my little Franciscan community that began in the South Bronx in 1987, talk about our Holy Father Saint Francis, Our Holy Mother Saint Clare, and Our Holy Aunt Mother Teresa. The reason we consider her part of our family is due to the profound influence she had on our community as a whole and on countless individual friars such as me. For many of us, our Franciscan vocation was born from an encounter with Mother Teresa and her sisters, the Missionaries of Charity.

In many ways, this woman, tiny in stature but a giant in holiness, gives us a privileged insight into what it might have been like to meet the Poor Man of Assisi in the thirteenth century or if Saint Francis walked the streets of the Bronx in the 1980s as Mother Teresa did. Like Saint Francis, she was little in the eyes of the world, but she would have an effect on the Church and the world that would ripple and ripple and ripple and will continue to ripple for centuries to come.

As my journey to Saint Francis began with Mother Teresa, so does this foreword. Now, on to the man whose way of life continues to be a privileged means of renewing and rebuilding.

Saint Francis never set out to change the world. Starting a religious order was not his idea. What was his desire? The wholehearted following of the Gospel and embracing of Christ crucified. Francis was focused on Jesus. He was focused on his own personal conversion and repentance. Everything else would flow from that. As Jesus himself said, "Strive first for the kingdom of God and his righteousness, and all things will be given you as well" (Mt 6:33).

This emphasis on Saint Francis's dedication to his personal conversion above all else should in no way be used to undercut the Church's teaching on social justice or her mission to actively be light and leaven in the culture, but it is a reminder of priority. It's a reminder of where our true power comes from and a reminder of what the world really needs. The power of the saints continues to renew the earth centuries after their death.

The world needs God. The world needs his grace, his truth, his mercy, and his zeal. The reason the saints are such powerful influences in the world and the reason that their power echoes for centuries after their earthly life has ended is because they communicate to the world, by word and deed, Jesus. They bring God to the world. And we can't give what we haven't received.

I had the great joy of beginning a friendship with the author of this book, Thomas Griffin, on a basketball court in New York City, where I had the privilege of helping him on his journey toward humility basket after basket. From there, various friars and I have had the joy of walking with Thomas and sharing our lives with him. Over the last few years, Thomas, his wife, and a couple dozen other lay people have been receiving formation from the friars on Saint Francis and how to live a Franciscan spirituality in the world.

The need for renewal in the world and the Church is obvious to all of us, but it is in no way new. As we are simply coming across the same old problems, but with slightly different manifestations in a different time period, our proposal is that we don't need to reinvent the wheel or seek out novelties for a remedy. The answer is always a return to Christ. Renewal is a work of God, and Saint Francis shows us in a beautiful and attractive way that renewal is possible and that the Father is faithful.

I'm grateful for the work that Thomas has put into studying Saint Francis and in writing this work, which authentically communicates Saint Francis and Franciscan spirituality. Most importantly, I'm grateful that this work has been a work of prayer and the fruit of his own ongoing conversion. For this reason, I believe that this book will not just communicate good ideas, but grace itself.

May the prayers of Our Holy Father Saint Francis, Our Holy Mother Saint Clare, and Our Holy Aunt Mother St. Teresa of Calcutta assist you as you strive to, as Saint Francis said, "hold back nothing of yourselves for yourselves, that he who gives himself totally to you may receive you totally."

Fr. Mark-Mary Ames, CFR
Franciscan Friars of the Renewal
April 2024

Introduction

M any of us view what is going on around us and don't know what to think or whom to believe. Much ink has been spilled decrying the current status of the Church, the United States government, and the overall culture in America. There have been sexual scandals in the Church. There is record low Mass attendance. Church leadership seems lost, and our culture rejects the value of the person. Society appears to be anti-God. It appears that all is lost. Our response is often despair, hopelessness, or uncertainty about what to do next. The answer, however, is right in front of us: The mess needs to be repaired. What is broken needs to be rebuilt.

The birth of this book resulted from my own brokenness.

One early September morning, I prayed in the school chapel before a beautiful and realistic crucifix, asking for forgiveness. I was reflecting on something that happened a few weeks prior to that morning. I had spoken to my wife in uncharitable ways and been, plain and simple, mean to her.

The morning after my words to her, I asked her to forgive

me and explained how sorry I was. She looked at me, hugged me, and forgave me without hesitation. I had gone to confession. Yet a few weeks later, sitting in that chapel, I still felt guilty. I had mended things with Joanna, but I was still beating myself up. My weakness brought me shame.

As I stared at the crucifix that morning, reflecting on my own brokenness, I was powerfully struck by something. Partially, it was a deeper realization of Jesus' suffering on the cross while pondering the depiction of his agony in front of me. His dead body hanging there seemed more real. His lifeless corpse carried a different kind of gravity.

Then, I understood. It was my sin that put him there. It was my weakness that was restored by his suffering. Jesus wanted me to be in that chapel to know and experience that he accepted me and loved me despite my flaws, and even because of them. For the first time, I realized that following him meant that I could expose my brokenness to him while knowing that he was not planning on leaving me unchanged.

I felt as if God was almost attracted to my brokenness, that my wounds gave him access to my heart in a new and more profound way. Then and there, for whatever reason, I thought of Saint Francis: the master rebuilder in the history of the Church. His humility and simplicity, and his focus on deep conversion, led generations of sinners to become saints. He knew that admitting one's own brokenness was a prerequisite for conversion. He knew that our wounds open us up for Christ's glory to shine.

Francis knew that Christ desired to jump into our brokenness by becoming one of us and that he replaced sin with his sacrificial love. That is valid theology. Francis, however, made me experience this truth incarnationally, concretely.

Before leaving chapel that morning, I outlined this book and decided to begin.

I am nowhere near an expert on the life of Saint Francis, nor am I a renowned scholar on the Franciscan charism or how this religious order has impacted the world and church history. But Francis has changed me. The journey of writing these words, as I hope you will experience yourself as you read, was a road to rebuilding what needs to be continually renewed in my own heart and life. It is about what Francis, and through him what Christ, has done to me.

The first step for repairing ourselves and our time is to acknowledge that we too are broken and in need of being rebuilt. I firmly believe that Francis wants us to know that conversion is a process. We are continuously being asked to begin again because we cannot save ourselves from sin.

Salvage for Renewal

In between teaching jobs, I entered the business sector for a year, working for a construction management firm as an estimator in New York City. Learning how to read blueprints was something completely new for me, but I threw myself into the task. There are so many different trades in every project: plumbing, electric, drywall, HVAC, flooring, and the list goes on and on. An important detail — often overlooked by some junior estimators — was a page containing the door schedule.

This is a page, usually toward the back of the blueprints, that lists every door on the job, along with its number and the work that was needed. Almost always you would see the words "furnish and install," which meant that a new door was to be purchased. However, what I quickly learned was that at the bottom of every blueprint page there was a notes section, in very small print. Not often, but sometimes, I would find the words "salvage" in that notes section regarding a certain door number. This meant that the client or architect wanted to keep the door, repair or paint as necessary, and use it again in their new space. Many estimators would miss this, and it would impact the price they quoted for our company to complete the work. Sometimes you could even find a note that said, "Salvage and reinstall all interior doors." Obviously, this could radically change the price of the project. This could be said for the notes section of any page, but the salvage wording was quite unique to the door schedule. At the beginning of a job an estimator could quickly assume that all doors needed to be new, that nothing of the old could remain.

Doing so would mean that they got it wrong.

Too often we can have the same perspective when we view the mess of our times and the imperfections of our institutional church. We are so fed up with how things are that we think, "All is lost. We need to dismantle everything and make it all new again." Our plans or blueprints include demolition, not restoration. We neglect to repair.

What I have seen in studying the life of St. Francis of Assisi (and in getting to know the Franciscan Friars of the Renewal) is that most of the time, all we need to do is salvage what we have already been given. All we need to do is bring to light what has always been there and what has always been true: Following Jesus Christ means I commit myself to a personally intimate, ongoing, and radical transformation of my heart to be in line with his heart. Being Christian means that we understand that our personal mess and the mess of the world are things that Jesus wants to and can salvage; that my commitment to my own ongoing conversion in Christ, and the commitment of every other person on the planet, is the answer to renewal.

Francis discovered that being a disciple meant that everything was about this repair mission. First, it was his own heart that needed to be healed. Only then could he bring the redeeming love of Christ's heart to every broken circumstance that he encountered. That is why he impacted the Church the way he did. That is why so many left their former ways of living to follow him. It was all about deep conversion, springing from the intimate encounter of his heart with the living flame of Jesus' heart. The life, witness, and message of St. Francis of Assisi is one of the best paths forward in bringing about faithful and lasting renewal in the Church and across America because it first acknowledges one's own weakness. Francis's manner of following after Christ did not bring about lukewarm faith, nor did it cause superficial belief. His dynamic effect on the Church did not make Christ's disciples flee from the world either. The true Franciscan spirit enlivened future centuries of disciples because those who followed his lead were unapologetically Christ-centered and unwaveringly driven to evangelize and sanctify the world.

Jesus famously asked Francis to "rebuild" his Church. Today, so many Catholics want our lives, families, nation, and Church repaired as well. If we investigate the details of what made Francis so unique and impactful, while practically revealing how we can channel the same power today, the result will be the creation of a deep renewal. This renewal, this repair mission, begins with individual conversion just as it did in the age of Saint Francis.

1
Francis and His Life's Work

Francis was only one person. By the time he died, he had started three religious orders — the Friars Minor for men, the Poor Clares for women, and an order for lay people. During his lifetime, nearly five thousand men dedicated their lives as friars. By the year 2000, the Franciscan Order included thirty-five thousand friars, one thousand sisters, and more than one million lay men and women.[1]

How did one person have such a huge impact? How did one man spark the beginning of so much good?

St. Francis of Assisi (1182–1226) is known by almost all Catholics and by a large portion of the worldwide population. Famously, he is recognized for two specific things. One is a personal attribute, and one is a statement. The first is true but an exaggeration; the second is a statement that has never been proven to be spoken by Francis. First, he is known for his love of animals. Most Catholic parishes host a blessing of animals service on or around his feast day on October 4. Second, Francis is purported to have said, "Preach the gospel always and when necessary, use words."

Unfortunately, many people characterize this great saint as a gentle animal-lover and an avoider of confrontation, rather than a disciple of Christ who was known for his radical preaching and way of life. The reason why the way of Saint Francis is not extremely well-known or practiced is because we have lost the true sense of who this man of intense faith really was.

Francis did live in the wilderness for a portion of his early life post-conversion. He did find God's beauty in everyday experience, which included nature. However, his main focus was not the birds of the air and the fish of the sea, but the souls that Christ thirsted for. This is the first step to renewal: to clarify who the man Francis was, so that we can better understand his purifying and extremely effective way of following Jesus.

What drew Francis into the heart of Jesus Christ was the all-encompassing nature of the message of the Gospel. Jesus demanded everything of those who followed him. In our times, so many can be quick to shave down the rougher edges of the gospel message to fit their own prerogatives. The truly Franciscan lens does no such thing. Everyone loves nature and finds beauty in creation, so statues of Saint Francis are found in countless gardens, and representations of his words are written in some secular places. When we get to know Francis, however, we see that most of his words (like those of Christ) were not easy to swallow. He consistently challenged the status quo.

The words recounted in the biographies of Francis convey the fact that Francis was known for his preaching. He urged his followers to speak up (using their words) to champion the beauty, power, and truth of Jesus' message. He was a witness, but he was also a messenger. His message, unlike many of his contemporaries and those of our age, always kept true to who he was and who Christ was calling him to be. Francis was a true instrument of peace, but many times his tools were words that cut to the heart, because he remained steadfast in his connection to Christ's mission.

Early Life and Conversion

Francis was born into a wealthy family. His father, Pietro, was a cloth merchant who traveled Europe frequently, making large sales in the finest cities. He would often revel in the beauty of France and decided to name one of his sons Francesco after his love for the country. Pietro firmly believed that his son would bring him even greater wealth because of Francis's great personality and energy. Francis was a normal, lively boy, but there remained something different about his heart even as he appeared to be sucked into worldly affairs.

While that inclination toward the good won out in the end, young Francis was not perfect. He was known to attend — and host — quite a few parties with his friends. Pope Pius XI noted that, "as a youth, St. Francis was expansive and high strung, a lover of luxurious dress. He was accustomed to invite to magnificent banquets the friends he had chosen from among the fashionable and pleasure-loving young men of the town."[2] The prior life of Francis, pre-conversion, was similar to that of his contemporaries. His former way of life would, in time, help him better understand what people were looking for in life. His past ways prepared him to become the saint that God was crafting him to be.

Francis's early aspiration was to one day become a knight. He had his chance to chase his dream in 1205 for Pope Innocent III, but not long into his journey he fell very ill. While recovering, he heard God's voice asking him a direct question: "Francis, who can do more for you, the lord or the servant?" Francis answered, "The lord." God replied: "Then why do you leave the lord for the servant, a rich lord for a poor man?" And Francis asked, "Lord, what would you have me do?" God said, "Return home and you will be told what to do."

Arriving back in Assisi as a changed man with a radically different view of the world around him, Francis was still on the road to finding his calling. He desired to serve the poor and provide aid to the outcast while diving deeper into a life of prayer. Interiorly, he had a negative and even repulsive view of the sick, especially lepers. "If we are to believe the chronicler, Matthew of Parish, there were no fewer than twenty thousand lepers in Europe at that time. Everywhere, one would run across these unfortunates, whose putrefying flesh, oozing ulcers, and pestilential odor brought disgust."[3]

In 1206 something changed inside of the great saint. Francis encountered a leper on the road, and instead of being revolted by the look of the man, he was drawn to give him what he had and to serve him in the moment. Francis's groundbreaking experience with the leper allowed him to see the sweetness of loving the lowly, and from that day, he was profoundly drawn to meeting Christ in the poor and sick. Francis later described this time period as personally transformative. It led him to view what was once bitter as sweet, and what was once sweet as bitter. Jesus was working within him, calling him to a deeper life within the heart of God.

Not long after this encounter, Francis was praying before the famous San Damiano cross when he received the calling that would ultimately change his life and the life of the Church. Christ spoke from the cross and said, "Francis, repair My house which, as you can see, has fallen into ruin." He would soon begin the process of literally repairing the San Damiano church building, which was physically falling apart, one stone and plank of lumber at a time.

The way of life that Jesus' invitation inspired in this man from Assisi quickly began to draw attention and followers. Men were drawn to his witness because it was so clearly connected to Christ. His way of life conveyed an authenticity and also an audacity that attracted people who were looking to devote the entirety of their being to God.

As his following increased exponentially, Francis started his own formal way of life, preparing a rule for a new religious order. In order to gain approval from the Vatican, Francis traveled to Rome to meet with Pope Innocent III. Englebert explains the beauty and power of Francis's proposal: "What the Rule is. It obliges the friars to conform to the kind of life imposed by Christ on his apostles, that is, the integral practice of the Gospel. In this lay its great and complete novelty, for never before had a monastic rule made the Gospel taken literally the foundation of the religious state."[4]

Reflecting on the proposal of such a religious order, the pope spoke with several cardinals. Some cardinals cried out that what Francis desired to create was not possible to live out through mere human strength. They were convinced that Francis was a holy man who could do so, but could his followers? Francis's plan was so simple that it somehow sounded impossible: he wanted to live a life similar to how Jesus lived with his disciples, and he wanted to live according to Jesus' precepts. This is what we are all called to do, but Francis decided to go for it with all of his strength. As one cardinal replied: "If we reject this poor man's request on such a pretext, would not this be to declare that the Gospel cannot be practiced, and so blaspheme Christ, its Author?"[5] Innocent III never forgot these words, and Francis's request was granted.

The earliest part of the Franciscan movement was spent in prayer, sacrifice, and service while his community rebuilt three church buildings and lived among lepers. After these were complete he realized that Jesus was not simply asking him to rebuild the wood, mortar, and brick of church buildings — he was being asked to repair the Body of Christ, which is the Church itself. That repair project would lead to the healing of countless lives.

Words to Be Defined By

One day after Mass, early on in his new way of life, Saint Francis decided to open up the Scriptures three times and draw out the Spirit's movements from this intentional openness to God's word. Some believe these passages were revealed over the course of time from attending daily Mass, but the manner in which he discovered them is not as important as the undeniable fact that he did. The three passages that he fell upon that day became the bedrock of the Franciscan community and the foundation for his repair mission.

The first passage was Jesus' words to the young rich man concerning what he was missing in order to enter eternal life: "If you wish to be perfect, go, sell what you have and give to [the] poor, and you will have treasure in heaven. Then come, follow me" (Mt 19:21). In their desire to give all to Christ, Francis and his religious brothers took Jesus' directive concerning poverty literally. Poverty was not just a nice option for following Jesus, but a necessary condition in being lowly and pouring oneself out as Jesus did (see Phil 2:6–8). After his conversion, Francis gave away all he had and desired to have as little as possible in his possession. His followers were invited to do the same, and one after another, lives were radically changed in the process.

The second passage Francis fell upon was Christ's words to his disciples when he was sending them out on a mission to proclaim the kingdom of God and to heal the sick: "Take nothing for the journey" (Lk 9:3). Bonaventure noted that when Francis heard this, he exclaimed: "This is what I above all things desire. This is what my whole heart craves."[6]

Material poverty is given an exclamation point by these words from Jesus. The journey being referenced is the pilgrimage that each Christian finds himself on, one that proclaims Jesus as God and his way as the truth. Francis was convicted of the fact that the path to holiness runs through poverty and simplicity. Pursuing a life of proclaiming poverty and simplicity to the world is not an option for Catholics, but rather a command from Christ. Dependence and trust must root the disciple as he goes about his duty of spreading Jesus' teachings, life, and salvific mission to a world that desperately needs him. Francis read this as directly applicable to his own life and circumstances.

The third and final passage Francis opened to was the Lord's words to his closest followers — known as the Conditions for Discipleship — following Peter's confession that Jesus was the Christ and the Son of God: "Whoever wishes to come after me must deny himself, take up his cross, and follow me" (Mt 16:24). Intimacy with and proximity to Jesus must be lived out through a sacrificial love that spares nothing.

Saint Bonaventure noted that Francis's call to rebuild the Church was given to him through this very channel of the cross. It was Jesus' suffering and suffocation on the cross that called Francis to radical discipleship. He wanted to take up what Jesus took up on that first Good Friday. Bonaventure writes, "In a lonely place, he became wholly absorbed in God. When Jesus Christ appeared to him under the form of a crucifix, at which sight his whole soul seemed to melt away; and so deeply was the memory of Christ's passion pressed on his heart, that it pierced even to the marrow of his bones. From that hour, whenever he thought upon the passion of Christ, he could scarcely restrain his tears and sighs."[7]

Francis teaches us that we should never complicate things or craft plans that overlook the essentials. Keep the main things, and from there we can live a life of transformative holiness. Those main things took a lifetime for Francis to investigate and contemplate. We must begin with them also.

The three passages above are rooted in poverty, simplicity, and sacrifice. In an organic manner, they provide the springboard for the four essentials Francis lived by: the Gospel, the poor, the Eucharist, and the Blessed Mother. The Scriptures provide the context for why we are made; a commitment to poverty and simplicity gives us access to the movement of Christ to save us; the Eucharist makes present the sacrifice that makes any other sacrificial love possible.

Catholics have heard of these four essentials. Some might hear them and claim that these basic steps are obvious — nothing new here. However, the life and dedication of Saint Francis reveal that these essentials take a lifetime to dive into. They provide a wellspring of profound and perpetual encounters that are meant to shake us at our core on a daily basis. If we think that we have them figured out and we understand their importance, we are not living as Francis did.

We are called to begin with them, live by them, and be forever changed by them.

The Gospel

Scripture was the home in which Saint Francis lived. Home is a place where we are loved and challenged; home is where the heart is; and this home is where Francis began each day.

Francis's move to open Scripture, somewhat randomly, and bind himself to what three passages proclaimed was not an act of hyper-devotional piety. The Bible is the revealed way that God decided to show us who he is and who we are. As the divinely inspired love letter to the world, Sacred Scripture stands as an everlasting resource from which we can draw directives for our life.

Francis knew deeply that reading a passage from the Bible is unlike reading from any other literary composition. In Scripture, God breaks through to the individual in a unique way depending on the person's needs and the dispositions of their heart. Francis knew this to be the case, so he was consistently attentive to how God was speaking to him through his word. Knowing the Bible and memorizing much of the Gospels enabled Francis to live from the firm disposition of who God was and who he was called to be. The Bible contains God's voice and message to the world. The better we know his message, the more exposed we become to God's personality and love. We can become more aware that God often chooses to operate in hidden and humble ways.

So often, our contemporary age dismisses the Bible as irrelevant, outdated, and purely mythological. People of all ages never even crack open the Scriptures because they assume that these negative views of the Bible simply must be true. As knowledgeable Catholics, we can provide the historical backgrounds for the books in the Bible and show how much of it contains history, not myth. The best recipe to combat skepticism regarding the Sacred Scriptures, however, is simply to pick them up and begin reading them. A firsthand experience of the depth of God's mercy and his unparalleled love throughout the history of the Jewish people and as revealed in the life of Christ will be the ultimate witness to the authenticity of the Bible.

That beautiful witness of the Trinity woven throughout the Bible inspired Francis to preach, and preach a lot! Since he was so familiar with God's word, he desired to break it open and make it accessible to everyone he met. God's voice tends to do that to those who listen to it. True conversion results in the urge to spread the truth of what you have experienced to the entire world because that truth (that Person) has changed everything for you. For this reason, reciting Scripture and making reference to it became utterly natural to Francis.

The vigor and clarity with which Francis preached allowed his listeners access to God through his words and zeal. His preaching voiced the truth in charity and challenged all who heard him, while remaining steadfast to the compassion behind the challenge. People experienced Jesus Christ through Francis's words — and we are invited to have the same impact.

The covenant that God made with Israel was the keystone for how Francis urged others in the truth without sounding callous to hardships. Before God gave the Ten Commandments or any other laws to follow, he first made a covenant with his people. The Lord specifically does not make a contract. A contract is made between two equal parties, and it has conditions — pay a price and receive a service. Covenants are radically different from contracts, because covenants are unconditional. No matter what the people would do to God or not do for God, he was never going to abandon them — never.

When we approach the Bible from this perspective, we see that words of encouragement or chastisement from God are meant to call his people closer to his heart. This is what Francis loved about the Scriptures. He saw them as completely connected to his everyday experience, and he viewed them as a channel that allowed him to reach Christ. Every word found in Scripture is encapsulated by God's unconditional promise to remain with and for his people. The closer we stay to him, the better we are. Not because God punishes us for denying him, but because staying with him is what we are made for.

That is precisely why a Catholic cannot distance himself from the life and words of Jesus found in the four Gospels and the words of Sacred Scripture. Doing so only widens the gap between humanity and Creator and makes it easier for us to sin. Within a chapter and a half in the Bible, God's mission becomes a rebuilding one, following Adam and Eve's decision to throw away intimacy with God at the Fall. Repairing the hearts he created is what God does for the remainder of Scripture. So many run from him, but his love remains steadfast. If we want to learn from the saint of Assisi, then we need to learn the Scriptures.

Christ heals the brokenness of the world in his miracles and mends the hearts of sinners as he travels from town to town. Francis knew Christ's mission was not confined to historical events, but a continuing mission in which he and his friars participated. When Jesus heals a leper, gives sight to a blind man, raises Lazarus, or calls the young rich man to follow him, he is also acting on us in a specific manner. As we digest all the words and actions of Jesus Christ in Scripture, our faith comes alive when we recognize the relational nature of the Bible and of our God. For this reason, the Gospels are timeless in their relevance and impact. Each generation can contemplate God's words and actions as spoken to and acted upon them. Each individual can return to certain passages over and over again throughout his life and hear Christ speaking and acting on him in a different manner depending on the needs of his heart at that moment.

The influence of the Gospels on the ministry of Francis is difficult to overstate. Knowing Christ through the Bible fed his soul for preaching and allowed him to have greater insight into the needs of the human hearts that found their way into his path. The Word of God was a shelter that he lived in. Studying and contemplating Jesus' encounters with others shows us who he is and how we should respond when human beings are in need of his love, mercy, forgiveness, and a call to repentance.

Francis urges us to spend more time with God's Word so that we can be schooled in how to live a life that will make us who we were created to be. Like the apostles, we are asked to partner with Jesus in his public ministry, participating in the drama of love, mercy, and justice that make up God's search to rebuild the whole human race, one soul at a time.

The Eucharist

While knowing Jesus through the Scriptures, Francis noted that "in this world I cannot see the Most High Son of God with my own eyes, except for His Most Holy Body and Blood." On the night before he died, Christ left humanity the Eucharist as his last will and testimony. Knowing that his death was within twenty-four hours, his number one desire was to not leave us orphans. Francis was, in a sense, addicted to the Lord — he had to be in the presence of the Eucharist as often as he possibly could. Everything he did moved from a desire not simply to know Jesus better or feel more intimately connected to Christ. He wanted to spend time with him, to "waste time" with God so that he could be transformed.

If we are willing to spend hours of our time on something, then it must be something that we value highly: sitting with your spouse on the couch, playing with your toddler, enjoying the beauty of nature. Francis sat for hours before Jesus, not because he wanted to get something from God but because he craved his Presence. He was known to describe his prayer before the Blessed Sacrament with the analogy of what a poor man does at a rich man's door or what a sick person does before a doctor. "I pray. I adore. I love," he said.

Francis understood that to serve a broken world and know what the person or group in front of us needs the most, we must have an intimate connection with the Eucharist because of the humility it breeds and the dependence on God that it fosters. Francis noted in a letter to his friars: "Behold, every day He humbles himself (Phil 2:8), just as when 'from royal thrones' (Wis 18:15) He came into the womb of the Virgin; every day He comes to us himself humbly appearing; everyday He descends from the bosom of the Father upon the altar in the hands of the priest."[8] When we immerse ourselves in our humble God, he transforms us and engrains in us a humility that is both attractive and holy.

When Christ traveled during his public ministry, he knew what people needed from him. Francis also gained this knowledge of the human heart by spending so many hours with Jesus in the Eucharist.

The capacity to read the person we encounter may be the most powerful and critical gift of a disciple who rebuilds the world. This was not magic or a guessing game for Francis; he was able to see the common desires of the human heart because he knew what humanity needed from his study and contemplation of Sacred Scriptures. He knew the recipe to satisfy that need through his intense intimacy with Jesus in the Eucharist.

The only manner in which we can see God while on earth is through the reality of the Blessed Sacrament. As Francis said, "We have and see nothing corporally of the Most High himself, in this age, except the Body and Blood."[9] Catholics know this, and so we revere Jesus Christ in the Eucharist, but it can be so easy to lose focus on him as we go through our everyday lives. Francis asks us to seriously consider the transcendent Presence that is held in the priest's hands at every Mass. Do we realize its true majesty? "Or are we ignorant," Saint Francis asked, "that we must one day come into His Hands?"[10] One of the major driving forces behind Francis's life of faith was the fact that one day we will live in the arms of the One whom we receive at Mass.

Francis's focus on the Eucharist also reveals his Incarnational worldview. He was consumed by the fact that God stooped down to become one of us so that he could win over our hearts. He was amazed that the God of the universe took a manger for a throne. The concrete, physical nature that God assumed allows us a beautiful contact with him that should leave us awestruck. This is why, as Saint Bonaventure noted, Francis could not keep himself away from the Eucharist. "His Burning Love for the sacrament of our Lord's body seemed to consume the very marrow of his bones, as he wondered within himself which most to admire — The condescension of that charity, or the charity of that condescension of our Lord."[11]

Any sincere and long-lasting conversion will come about

through a radical focus on the Eucharist. Not just because human beings are made for worship and not just because Jesus told us to remember him in the Mass — but simply because the Eucharist is Jesus. Healing begins by being consumed in the fire of the Divine Healer, present to us in a real, life-changing way.

The Poor

After hearing Christ's words to "take nothing with you on the journey," Francis moved to "shape his life in all things according to the strict rule of apostolic poverty. From this day forward the man of God began, by divine inspiration, to strive after evangelical perfection."[12] Every decision he made in his life was now driven by the desire for a deeper encounter with God and others. For this reason, poverty brings about perfection: We are able to embrace an attribute of God himself. Making contact with God's willingness to be poor for our sake made Francis shine with the presence of God.

Saint Francis experienced true poverty in his encounter with the leper in Assisi. The leper was an outcast from society, but he was also materially poor. Through this encounter with the leper, Francis made it his life's work to be present to those who were in the midst of brokenness, pain, and loneliness. He lived in poverty and surrounded himself with the poor, choosing to be poor himself in order to mirror the nature of Christ's humility. He saw poverty as the invitation to "be perfect, just as your heavenly Father is perfect" (Mt 5:48).

When Francis visited the pope to receive approval for the initiation of a religious order, he found himself uncertain about what to say. He threw himself into hours of prayer, asking for how to explain his mission and calling. Finally, when he visited with the pope, he recited this message:

There is no fear, that the children and heirs of the Eternal King should perish with hunger, who by the power of the Holy Ghost have been born of a poor mother, and bear the image of Christ the King, being born by the spirit of poverty, in a religion of poverty. If, therefore, the King of Heaven has promised His followers an eternal kingdom, how much rather will He provide them with those things which He is wont to impart indifferently to the evil and the good?[13]

Franciscan poverty is concerned with this utter reliance on God. Francis knew that the great and powerful King would provide for his needs and those of his brothers. This was a process for Francis, who grew up in a wealthy family and was exposed to the finer things in life. We know that lepers used to repulse him. We know that he used to host huge parties with amazing food and drink. Yet poverty became a part of his DNA after he had his pivotal encounter with Jesus on the cross in the church of Saint Damian. Experiencing Jesus, poor on the cross, made Francis desire poverty in its truest sense — an imitation of Christ's own life and an absolute recognition of God's providence — not simply words about how the poor should be cared for or how humility is a virtue.

We cannot overexaggerate the deep connection between the inclination we should have to serve the poor, and our own personal sin. Saint Francis declared, "A man sins, who wants rather to receive from his neighbor, what he does not want to give of himself to the Lord God."[14] If a Christian does not have contact with the material poor, there is something missing not only in his relationship with others but also with God. Not because we are breaking a "rule," but because we are missing out on gaining access to a critical aspect of God's nature.

For this reason, Francis desired to remove any barrier between himself and others; he deeply wanted to hand over to God all that he was. Francis wanted to waste his life on being poor and on spending time with the poor because that is what Jesus did — that is who Jesus is. Being poor, in some way, and serving the poor is a requirement for every disciple.

The service to the poor that the Franciscans live out is not a service project or a movement to help a lower class of human beings. Franciscans also do not serve the poor to merely live out a worldly sense of "being nice" or "kind." The poor reveal something deeper about the human condition — our dependence on God — that all people, especially Christians, must come to grips with. That is why Francis was so radical about poverty. That is why Franciscans live out poverty rather than just serve the poor. Francis, in fact, loved poverty so much that he called it "Lady Poverty" and referred to it like a princess that he served with every fiber of his being.

After Francis had come to seek the approval of the pope and made his appeal to serve the poor through his religious order, the pope had a dream about Francis. He saw a poor and simple man in the midst of the crumbling buildings of the Vatican. The poor man was holding up the ruins on his shoulders. Then the pope heard these words concerning the poor man: "Truly, this is he who by his works and his teachings shall sustain the Church of Christ."[15]

Saint Francis accomplished heroic deeds and lived a life of radical devotion. His actions helped change the world. However, it was the divine roots of his actions that truly made the impact. It was his simple imitation of the God who emptied himself out to be poor that renewed the earth. This is beautifully emphasized in the *Catechism of the Catholic Church*'s explanation of poverty:

> In its various forms — material deprivation, unjust oppression, physical and psychological illness and death — human misery is the obvious sign of the inherited

condition of frailty and need for salvation in which man finds himself as a consequence of original sin. This misery elicited the compassion of Christ the Savior, who willingly took it upon himself and identified himself with the least of his brethren. Hence, those who are oppressed by poverty are the object of a preferential love on the part of the Church which, since her origin and in spite of the failings of many of her members, has not ceased to work for their relief, defense, and liberation through numerous works of charity which remain indispensable always and everywhere.[16]

Being poor and living simply makes one more alive. Francis viewed discipleship as a life-or-death endeavor. He loved the words of Saint Paul: "Now those who belong to Christ [Jesus] have crucified their flesh with its passions and desires" (Gal 5:24). Bonaventure noted that in order "to clothe his body with the armor of the Cross, he began to exercise such severe discipline over all his sensual appetites, that he hardly took such food as was necessary for the support of his nature."[17] Francis's many practices of abstinence and sacrifice were done out of his radical sense of poverty and his dependence on God for absolutely everything.

Without mentioning these and many other ways that Francis was intensely poor, we would miss out on who the man truly was. For him, it was impossible to say that you are a follower of Jesus if you did not have contact with the material poor. Perhaps more than anything else, we must understand his reckless falling in love with poverty if we desire to know the heart of Francis and the way that he changed the world.

The Blessed Mother

Where Jesus is, there is his mother. Francis saw the role of Mary as indispensable for the disciple because of how deep her love was for her son and for him. Francis did not show devotion to the Blessed Mother out of a formality. He had a relationship with Mary. He experienced her presence and love on a daily basis. She was another mom to him.

As he began his new way of life, he desired to remain close to Mary always. One of the churches that he physically rebuilt was St. Mary of the Angels at the Portiuncula, which became a sort of home base for Francis. Bonaventure notes that "this place was loved by the holy man above all places in the world, for here, in great humility, he began his spiritual life; here he grew in virtue; here he attained his happy and perfect end; and this, at the hour of his death, he commended to his brethren as a spot most dear to the Blessed Virgin."[18] This little chapel became the birthplace — the cradle — of the Order of Friars Minor.

Francis grew in his conversion in the arms of his mother. He spent much time in the church of St. Mary of the Angels as he began to outline how he desired to live for Christ. He sat there, "pouring forth continual prayer to her who had conceived the Word, full of grace and truth, that she would ... be his advocate; and now, by the merits of that Mother of Mercy, he conceived and brought forth the spirit of evangelical truth."[19] Through Mary, who conceived the Truth in her very person, he came to know what it meant to be truly Christian, and he depended on her guidance throughout his life.

A special dedication and devotion to the Blessed Mother is asked of all who follow in the shadow of Saint Francis, because she is a necessary part of the salvation of the world and the redemption of the human heart. She was the first one to feel the presence of the Savior of the world on earth when he was in her womb. Mary and Joseph were the first human beings to cast their eyes on God made man. They were the ones to form Jesus as a boy and guide him as a young man, and Mary was the one who comforted him in his dying moments. Her faith and witness to the Body of

Christ influences the entire mission of the Church. This is a deep theological truth that Francis experienced in his inner being.

Mary reveals to humanity that God can do incredible things with those who give their hearts to him. The little ones can become the ones who rebuild humanity. Francis depended on her aid and desired to view the heart of Christ through her eyes, so he meditated on her relationship with Christ continuously.

The Franciscan Rosary (also called the Franciscan Crown or Seraphic Roasary) has been worn around the waist of many of the friars for generations as a reminder of Mary's role in the life of the disciple and how we should rely on her guidance. Mary is, in a sense, what holds up the Franciscan and binds him to the Lord. We must also be bound to Christ through the intimacy that only Mary can deliver to us. She carried God to her cousin Elizabeth (see Lk 1:39–56). She held Christ when he was taken down from the cross after his death. The road to renewal will only occur when we each accept the invitation to reform our lives and, like Mary, carry God to everyone whom we encounter. The process of bearing the love of the Trinity and sharing it with the world is one that should humble us, invite us into poverty, and allow us to give birth to the conversion of others.

Along with his mother, Christ decided to "choose poverty," says Saint Francis.[20] We must also become poor, because the only human being to ever live and not sin was poor, and because God intentionally chose to become poor in order to bring about life. When we enter into this poverty of the Holy Family, we will become like God — we will become more than we ever thought we could be.

Like all other aspects of the way of Saint Francis, becoming like Christ means that we live for others rather than ourselves. Francis noted that each of us has the responsibility to share the message and life of Christ. The saint of Assisi once told his friars, "If the Blessed Virgin is so honored, as is right, because she car-

ried Him in (her) most holy womb ... just and worthy ought he
be who handles with hands and receives with heart and mouth
and offers to others to be received Him, who will die no more."[21]

Today, we receive the Eucharist in the palm of our hands, on
our tongue, and into our bodies. We carry Jesus just like Mary did.
Every single time Francis received the Eucharist, he was shaken to
the core by that truth. He allowed her Immaculate Heart to shine
a light on his path toward rebuilding God's kingdom, and her holiness gave him the capacity to be healed of his wounds and then
bring about holiness in the lives of everyone else he encountered.

All that we have covered in this chapter is meant to help us begin to experience Saint Francis in a new and more profound way.
The truth of who he was should not leave us unchanged, and his
radical faith should challenge us to the core. Let us make Sacred
Scripture a home we reside in. A day shouldn't go by that we do not
contemplate some of God's words. Let us deepen our relationship
with the Gospel, poverty, the Eucharist, and the Blessed Mother.
Let these be the chorus of our life in a visible way. Let us begin
to see that following in the footsteps of Francis, who followed so
closely in the footsteps of Christ, is the way of the true disciple.

Reflect

- How can you grow your connection to the poor, the Blessed Mother, the Scriptures, or the Eucharist in light of what
  Francis said?
- How would you summarize your faith life? How do you
  want it to grow?
- Francis is misunderstood. How do you think people view
  you? Could your outside appearance or attitude be more
  aligned with the reality of your heart?
- Based on what you found to be most powerful from the life
  of Francis, what is something you can begin doing today to
  become more like him and more like Christ?

2
The Francis Way

Saint Francis radically changed the world. We know that his order exploded during his lifetime and in the following generations. This was a fact because of the friars' impact on their contemporaries but also because

> Francis was responsible for introducing and fostering many devotions and practices that have characterized Roman Catholicism for the last 800 years: Eucharistic Adoration, devotion to the Immaculate Virgin Mary, the Christmas creche and Christmas carols, devotion to Christ's passion, public preaching, and the promotion of the life of devotion and good works among the laity.[1]

Franciscans were at the tip of the spear of renewal because they were so involved in the ordinary experience of the Christian. They were present to the poor, and they were living in the communities. For this reason, their witness led others to fall in love with Christ and give their lives to him as well. This created a large impact on other mendicant orders. Most prominently, Saint Dominic started his religious order in 1216, six years after Saint Francis founded his. About forty years later the Augustinians were founded. While all these religious orders have particular charisms, there is no doubt that the life and intensity of Francis's faith also impacted the formation of these groups. The saint of Assisi was a simple man who desired to simply follow what Christ asked. That spark caught fire in Europe, and its fire still burns across the world today.

In his early life, Francis appeared to be an ordinary boy and young man. Yet an underlying difference set him apart. Surrounded by affluent families during his upbringing, he found a certain appeal in their lifestyle. However, deep within, he harbored a longing for a different kind of treasure. As Saint Bonaventure noted, "He knew not yet how he was to purchase it, nor what he was to give for it; only it seemed to be known to him that the spiritual Merchant must begin with the contempt of the world and the soldier of Christ must begin by victory over himself."[2]

In an introduction to *The Writings of St. Francis of Assisi*, Pope Pius XI begins by focusing on the times in which Francis lived. The problems that Francis faced in the culture and Church of his time are really no different than what we currently encounter. Too often, we can convince ourselves that our age is the worst in the history of the Church. However, every age is similar in its troubles, and each time period truly has the same remedy.

Heresy is a strong word that is used sparingly in our age, but heretical ideas (false teachings) have recently had profound effects on the Church and the culture. In the time of Francis, Pope Pius XI noted, "heresies gradually arose and grew … propagated either by open heretics or by sly deceivers."[3] In the same way, today we have those who outright defame the teachings of Christ and those, within the Church herself, who use their own words to deceive the masses into believing incorrect teachings. Both the heretic with the megaphone and the one with the humble smile must be answered by those who wish to rebuild and repair the world, because it is the truth that will set us free. Pius XI noted that "heretics" desire to reform the Church and the culture by presenting something different than what the Gospel has always proclaimed. These outright rebellions against Church teaching frequently lead to rebellions against the state. In Saint Francis's time, as in ours, these individuals were going about their own projects and were more concerned with their own egos than with bringing about true reform in the Church.

That is why we must always reflect on the purpose of our repair project. In our desire to help repair the world around us, it is critical that we bring our motives to the level of Christ, the Good Shepherd, who always leads by knowing his flock and calling them by name. Leaders of virtuous reform are always obedient to Christ and his Church, and they are always most occupied with serving souls out of love, not pride, ego, or personal gain.

Continuing his description, the pope wrote, "Although the Catholic faith lived in the hearts of men, in some cases intact and in others a bit obscured, however lacking they have been in the spirit of the gospels, the charity of Christ had become so weakened in human society as to appear to be almost extinct."[4] There were more warm bodies in the churches of Francis's time than there are in ours, and there were more people who professed the Faith, but there was something pivotal missing: There was a lack of deep intimacy with the person of Jesus Christ.

Today, our churches are not as full as they once were, but we do have plenty of children enrolled in religious education and many who have contact with our parishes through our schools and other initiatives. Yet they are not alive with the vigor that an intentional disciple embodies. We know this is the case because so many stop attending Mass and parish events once they receive first holy Communion and Confirmation. We also know that many families enrolled in Catholic schools do not attend Mass on a regular basis.

Catholics are real in name, but not so much in practice. To be like Christ is our anthem, and yet so many blend into the culture, not allowing the light of Christ to shine brightly through their words and actions. There were great saints during the time of Saint Francis, but by all appearances the love of Christ as lived out by the people appeared to be "extinct." The present moment also appears inundated with souls who live out their own affairs above everything else without regard for others. The love of Christ urged Francis to reform this inclination of the human heart. He desired for all people to hear God's voice and not have hardened hearts. That process began through a softening of his own heart.

In order to travel on the way of Francis, we must begin by examining our own faith lives to decipher whether or not we are lacking intimacy with the Lord, as so many people were in the time of this great saint of Assisi. It is rather easy to point out statistics on Mass attendance and belief in the Eucharist, but what about our own relationship with Jesus Christ? Can we shift our speech to speak to him more frequently and with more of a focus on him as a person who is alive and relevant for our lives? Can we move to inject God more into our lives in an organic way so that others can also encounter him in the process?

There was also "constant warfare carried on by the partisans of the Empire ... and by those of the Church," Pope Pius XI noted.[5] Tribalism in party politics is nothing new, and neither is its negative impact on a country's citizens. Arguments from "the left and the right" are heard in the halls of the capitol, in the living rooms of ordinary Americans, and in parish rectories across the nation. Too often the verbal warfare is meant to simply make the other side look bad rather than speak the truth with compassion.

Francis's age was filled with physical disputes as well. At times this played out in the divide and antagonism that existed between the nobility and the rising merchant class. The Faith was so ingrained in society at that time that disputes inside the Church spilled out into the public square. Too many Christians operated from a place of hatred rather than operating from an experience of a personal relationship with Jesus Christ. There was constant warfare between parties of the Empire as well as factions inside the Church. "Horrible massacres, conflagrations, devastation and pillage, exile, confiscation of property and estates were the bitter fruits of these struggles."[6]

While Francis's age contained awful massacres, our time is consumed by endless verbal disputes that take place on social media and in the newsrooms of major television networks. If we want true reform, we must focus on the topics and realities that will actually change the lives of real individuals. We are not meant to shy away from every dispute, but we are asked to disarm evil with good. This is not fairy tale language, but literally the message of Jesus Christ himself, which Saint Francis championed. Fighting evil with love is not an invitation to wear rose-colored glasses. Sacrifice works. Love does prevail. All we need to do is tap into its power.

No one could argue against the tremendous similarity between Francis's age and ours when it comes to the fact that a vast majority of the people "allowed themselves to be overcome by egotism and greed for possessions and were driven by an insatiable desire for riches."[7] The worship of the self is the poison of our time, and it was the major contributing factor to the darkness surrounding the moral fiber of the thirteenth century.

People sought to satisfy their greed and desire for pleasure at all costs. Fortunes were piled up and done so in sinful manners, "sometimes by the violent extortion of money and other times by usury."[8] Similar to our age, many people in the time of Francis were most concerned with selfish pride and comfort; nothing else was seen as important.

Pius XI noted that "a much stronger flame of light and love was necessary to reform human society which had been so profoundly disturbed."[9] Since Francis was surrounded by riches and luxury as a youth, he was better able to speak to its danger as well as its remedy. Once he decided not just to hear the Gospel, but act on it, "he had decided to never deny help to the poor."[10] Dropping one's own ego on the ground and refusing to worship at the altar of self-comfort is the only way to do that.

He walked away from his former ways and clung to a new road, which would lead to a renewal of his heart and life. This is the core of the Christian life. This was the primary repair mission that Francis was invited into by Christ. Encountering Jesus means that he radically changes us, especially the aspects of ourselves that seem unredeemable. Each and every one of us has had moments in our lives when we doubted whether or not change was possible — real change that would actually make circumstances better. So many people might convince themselves that "renewing the Church" is blind sentimentality. Many might say this is an impossible task. Maybe there is too much wreckage?

The way of Francis offers something so much more than lip service to a newly paved road of existence. Deep down, all husbands, wives, mothers, fathers, priests, and religious want to be set afire with a new path forward. We do not want our life just to be "different"; we want to be changed forever so that we can move ahead with different hearts. Deep down, we all want greatness. This is how Francis wants to speak to the average American Catholic who is going about his or her ordinary life. Deep within, we might feel too normal or simple to alter the course of history. Yet Francis was inspired, through the words and actions of Christ, to dream of a world set ablaze by the small spark that he could provide. Repairing the world simply requires that we accept the real possibility that we are all sparks waiting to be ignited for God's glory.

Saint Bonaventure once said that Francis "seemed like a burning coal alive with the fire of God's love."[11] You could see it in his eyes, hear it in his words, and feel it when you were in his presence. His passion for Christ urged others to respond likewise. This is yet another providential detail that ought to spur us forth to strongly consider the way of Saint Francis as the best road forward. His issues were similar, so we should consider his response as valid because of the vast impact he had on the people of his age and the generations that followed him. Our rebuilding must begin like his.

His Words Show the Way

One Christmas, my friend Andrew and his family visited my wife and me. At the time, their son Damian was only two months old, and his older brother, Dominic, was a little over two years old. Damian was diagnosed with RSV in the weeks leading up to the visit, but doctors said the family was fine to travel. We had a nice dinner, the boys went to sleep, and we ended up staying up late talking and having a drink. When it was time for bed, Joanna and I took the couch and allowed Andrew and his wife to sleep in our room with their boys.

At around 2:00 a.m. I heard Andrew's wife spring from the bedroom to the hallway. Then I heard the shower go on. I got off the couch and heard Andrew screaming to Emily, "Did you call? We need to call. Call 911."

When I opened the bathroom door, he had Damian's head bent into the shower stall to allow the steam from the hot water to enter his nose. Andrew looked me straight in the eyes and said, "He is not breathing. His lips are turning purple. Call 911."

I called and then ran out into the parking lot of our apartment complex. It was a freezing cold December night. Within two minutes the ambulance arrived, and the paramedics had Damian hooked up to oxygen, his small body lying on a massive stretcher. We went to the hospital together, and after roughly twelve hours of monitoring, Damian was released from the hospital with no complications or injuries.

In those two minutes that I waited for the ambulance in that freezing parking lot, the only thing I could think to say to God was, "Please, help him. Help Damian. Help him." It was one of the most desperate prayers of my life. The idea of prayer and the notion of God's existence was never so real for me.

Andrew's words that night and the way he looked at me when he told me to call 911 will be forever burned into my memory. It was the look of a dad, worried to death about his son. It was the look of a friend who desperately needed my help. His words showed me the way. They also revealed our complete and utter need for God. If we are really honest, we need God for everything. When Damian's life hung in the balance, nothing was more evident to me. To this day I still wonder, why can't I live from this truth every single day?

That is the beauty of a saint like Francis. He lived in such a way that he always remained focused on just how real his need was for God's loving care. The clarity I had about my need for God on that cold night was a clarity Francis had each day. Meeting Francis radically changed people's hearts because of the lengths to which he went to stay true to Jesus' transformative words and actions. Being Catholic, saying his prayers, and being a man of faith was not about getting what he wanted when things were tough, but about a mode of existence. Being a man or woman of faith means that we are deeply aware of our complete dependence on God for everything. From this standpoint we can become a disciple who cooperates with God's desire to make us like his Son.

To meet Francis was, in a way, to encounter the living God.

This meant that he was not living in the abstract ether of spirituality, but in the soil of people's real lives. The perspective he had for life and for the soul in front of him led Francis to a manner of living that was inspiring and attractive. We can easily lose sight of the fact that holiness is the most authentic and most transformative way of life. Giving everything to Christ in trust will not leave us empty but will satisfy the deepest longings of our hearts.

When he spoke, his words were intensely radical, but his message was delivered with a specific look toward the other — a look of love, compassion and truth. He had given up so much, but he gained everything in return because he became small; he broke open every aspect of his life to God. Mothers and fathers know this logic when they choose to sit on the floor and play with their children. Giving into this small poverty makes us realize that it is in handing over our attention and time that we are given the greatest of gifts. When we turn our phones on silent and give our full attention to our child, it makes us more alive. Doing so actually allows us to be renewed in our heart and to see a side of ourselves and our children that is priceless.

Francis knew this simple secret about the human heart, so he wrote: "For men lose everything, which they abandon in this age; yet they carry with them the wages of charity and the alms, which they have given, because of which they will have from the Lord a reward and worthy recompense."[12] The loss of giving away possessions or worldly success is real and it is not to be quickly dismissed. Jesus demands everything of those who follow him. "Whoever is not with me is against me, and whoever does not gather with me scatters" (Mt 12:30). Therefore, we must give Christ our complete selves, but the reward will be greater than what is sacrificed. This is the beauty of discipleship. We are not to follow him so that we can receive spiritual trophies, but following him will lead to everlasting joy and peace. Like any fruitful relationship, we are devoted to the person out of love, but that love fills us unlike anything else.

This is great to read about, but sometimes life gets in the way of living this out. Have you ever felt the weight of carrying a relationship or responsibility that you knew was right, but it would cost you in some way? At times, it might even be a burden to carry your faith because of where you work or what your family thinks. The weight of doing what is right, what is best for us, is real and often burdensome. Remaining steadfast to the truth, to justice, to love requires sacrifice. Francis knew this well. Carrying that weight, in our families and in public, always liberates us and others (even if we cannot perfectly see it from our perspective).

We ought to love those with whom we have profound relationships, but that love is meant to extend to how we treat everyone. Francis radically loved his fellow brothers. He called his friars to treat strangers as if they were brothers. Extravagant love and mercy must be the rule, not the exception. His challenge was "that there be no friar in the world, who has sinned, as much as one could sin, that, after he has seen your eyes, never leaves without your mercy. And if he would not seek mercy, you are to ask him if he wants mercy. And if afterwards he would have sinned a thousand times before your eyes, love him more than me for this, so that you draw him to the Lord."[13]

We will fall, others will fall, but we must consistently return to the well of forgiveness. How do we look at those who are sinners? Following Francis — that is, following Jesus — is not a program of action that will lead to inevitable change as we would envision it. Christianity is a lesson in how to look at others and how to view the world. Christianity is a way of viewing the world that places the perspective of Christ at the forefront of everything that we are. The world needs repentance and renewal because it has gone astray. Jesus came to find the lost sheep, and now it is our turn to, like Francis, draw them to Christ through our gaze.

Francis called on his friars to love the perpetual sinner more than they loved Francis, their spiritual head. A modern equivalent would be to tell a husband to love the sinner at work more than his wife, or for a mother to love the nasty cashier more than her own daughter. The way of Francis is strikingly similar to the way of Jesus Christ because it counters the way we humans normally think and act. "For as the heavens are higher than the earth, / so are my ways higher than your ways, / my thoughts higher than your thoughts" (Is 55:9).

Jesus tells parables exactly for this reason. He desires to shake the cobwebs out of our heads and show us how to view the world differently. Because we do not know, properly, what it means to see the other as the other; to forgive in the manner in which we have been forgiven; to love without counting the cost and without caring what others think. This is the way of heroic holiness. This is what repairs the brokenhearted and allows dead souls to rise to new life. This is the logic of the empty tomb that shatters all darkness and despair.

The aforementioned path is not an escape to a world that only contains pleasantries and no conflict. Jesus demands that we show mercy. "For as you judge, so will you be judged, and the measure with which you measure will be measured out to you" (Mt 7:2). This does not mean that we cannot judge objective actions as right or wrong — we must do that, and so did Saint Francis. However, we must always place the need of the soul as a priority on our radar. The power of Christ can renew the heart of any sinner, no matter how great. If we do not believe this, we are actually anti-Christian.

Francis even noted that if a friar has committed mortal sin, his brothers should "not shame him nor utter detraction, but let them have great mercy upon him and keep very private the sin of their brother."[14] Forgiveness is the route that will lead to repentance, because it disarms even the proudest of sinners. A habitual move toward mercy and compassion will allow the disciple the true capacity of being a vessel for Christ's grace to work with and through. If the success of Francis teaches us anything, it must be that we are to be emptied so that the love and mercy of Jesus can work through us.

In speaking to priests and to those friars who wished to be priests, Francis stressed mercy, and he asked them to pay very close attention to the details of worship in a way that led not to heightened rules and idiosyncrasies, but to sanctification. For priests celebrating Mass, Francis counseled them with the following words: "Let every will, as much as grace helps it, be directed to God, desiring for that reason to please solely the Most High Lord himself."[15] Many people today misunderstand Francis, believing he was all about birds and dogs and feelings. While he loved the animals and understood the human experience, more often than not, he spoke about the will and the need to build strong habits.

At Mass, the priest and all those in attendance must move their minds to offer perfect praise to the Father. Our direction is toward Christ, who gave his life for you and for me. So we are called to break our hearts open just like his heart, which was broken on Calvary for you and for me. The writings of Francis show this beautiful dance between emulating the actions and life of Christ while showing that this is meant to bring the disciple to worship more powerfully.

Contemplating and living out Jesus' mission means that this is the only way to respond to the fragile nature of our own hearts and the broken status of the human condition. Most critically, our worship at Mass will give us the strength to speak the good news in our life. When we receive the Word of God, we can better speak the truth of God. Worthy reception of the

Eucharist will make the most practical difference, if we understand what holy Communion actually is. More than anything else, Francis's writings and words highlight that Christ is the center, and that our central focus needs to be on him and what he wants to do to us.

Lastly, if we are going to speak for and about Christ, we need to know how to do so. When the friars would preach, Francis urged them to have "brevity of speech — since a brief word did the Lord speak upon the Earth" (Rom 9:28).[16] Here, he was speaking of formal preaching, but that does not dismiss laymen and women from our duty to preach the Gospel as well. When we have the opportunity to share the truth and love of Christ at work, in school, or at family gatherings, we should follow the brevity of Francis. The mission of the apostle is to be short but powerful in his or her words.

Like Francis and the friars who "gave all that they possibly had," we must also strive to lay down all that we are at the feet of Jesus Christ because real transformation across society begins with the individual.[17] So we begin anew each day.

Repentance Is the Key

Fr. Benedict Groeschel, who helped found the Franciscan Friars of the Renewal (CFRs), once wrote, "The Christian life is a process of repentance and reform leading to renewal."[18] Repentance is impossible without humility and simplicity. Francis desired to be a "new fool for Christ" with his unwavering focus on humility and simplicity. This would not change because it could not change; this, in summary, is the Gospel.[19] Any road of revival must be paved with these non-negotiable elements.

Beneath all movements to create a better world or craft a more Christian society must be the eradication of the view that being religious simply means that we are nice to everyone. So much of my motivation to write this work comes from hearing and witnessing this attitude. Today, too many people think of Jesus and Saint Francis as simply "nice," and they equate following them with being nice. We worry that telling a person he or she is wrong means we are judging that person and being mean. Yet the truth is that Francis was not just nice to people. Neither was Jesus.

We are called to be more than nice, and we are asked to be more than actors who do and say the right thing at the right time. We are invited to have the love of a person be our anthem and our joy. Yes, we should desire change, wholesome and virtuous renewal, but it can never be stripped from the cord that binds us to looking Jesus in the face as we vow to quench his thirst for souls. Jesus is the prototype; he is the litmus test for renewal. The words of Christ were not always nice. He was rooting out sin and evil. He was concerned with changing people's lives.

We all need to reject sinful ways. Only as each of us does so can we experience renewal of the larger society. The Incarnation reveals the fact that God desires to sit with every sinner, one at a time. Conversion is the result of intimacy. Jesus travels from town to town, and he spends time with the sick and the outcasts to show that no one is past saving, and everyone deserves his attention.

On several occasions in the Gospels, the Greek word used for Jesus "healing" someone is *therapeuo*. This word does not mean a magical fixing, but a curing that also embodies hands-on, time-consuming service. Christ spent intentional time with every person he healed. He never rushed, and he never overlooked the profound dignity of the individual in front of him. Salvation comes to us through the one God-man, and it passes from him to the first disciples down through the generations. Christianity is a causal chain of individual people who have been radically touched by the gaze, words, and actions of Jesus Christ. That encounter pushes disciples to desire to serve others by spending intentional and powerful time with them as well — calling them to live life to the fullest.

Being nice does not sum up the mission of Jesus or Francis, because there were many times when the person they were ministering to needed to change their ways. God desired to free them from actions or circumstances even if they did not see it themselves. The Pharisees and Jewish hierarchy did not think Jesus was nice because he called them out and asked them to change. On occasion, those listening to the sermons of Francis and his friars received sharp words, not fuzzy and warm platitudes. Sometimes the truth does not bring acceptance, but that does not mean we stop preaching. The truth will set people free, even when it is hard, because Jesus is the truth. Francis knew this deeply.

The Lord's presence causes people to change their ways because that is what holiness does. It is both attractive and purifying. The very first words spoken by Jesus in the Gospel of Mark concern repentance. "This is the time of fulfillment. The kingdom of God is at hand. Repent, and believe in the gospel" (Mk 1:15). To repent (the Greek word is *metanoia*), to change your life (even the way you think) or set forth in a new direction, is the entire point. This is not a self-help program or a recipe to becoming happier than you ever thought you could be. Following Jesus is about seeing all that you were made for and having your relationship with him shine forth through every aspect of your life.

After the crowds witness the coming of the Spirit and the preaching of the apostles at Pentecost, they ask what they ought to do as a result of this message and event. Peter tells them, "Repent and be baptized, every one of you, in the name of Jesus Christ for the forgiveness of your sins; and you will receive the gift of the holy Spirit" (Acts 2:38). The entire Christian message and life began with one person, Jesus Christ, and his twelve followers. One-by-one conversions by Jesus and his message eventually changed the world.

St. Francis of Assisi, in effect, did something similar, but it was based solely on his desire to be like Christ. He frequently spoke and wrote about how the friars were called to walk "in the footprints of Christ." Picture a field of snow that only one person has walked through. If Francis knew that Jesus was the one who passed through this field, he would have placed his foot inside each footprint exactly the way Jesus did. This is how he desired to follow the words and life of Christ. He wanted it to be as if he were living with Jesus and the disciples during his public ministry.

This is a fine distinction that we must pay close attention to: Intentional disciples of Jesus change the world because they are close to and know the person of Jesus Christ on a profound interior level that impacts all spheres of their life. Christians do not change the world because Jesus changed the world or even just because Jesus commanded his apostles to go out and make disciples. Disciples change the world because they are first changed, and they see how that change has made them into the men and women whom they were created to be.

To rebuild the world means we first look at our own brokenness. The wounds of our own hearts and the hearts of the rest of the world ought to be named so they can be renewed.

We are not concerned with mere philanthropy or self-help and wellness practices. Renewal is about bringing souls back to God because they belong to him. Belonging to him means that we are the ones who live his love as part of our very nature. Truly, this means that we become like Mary (the first disciple and a true mother figure to Francis). This is why the great biblical writer Erasmo Leiva-Merikakis writes that "the deepest vocation of the world and of society is to become the divine vessel that the Virgin already is. She is the archetype of redeemed creation."[20]

Holy ones bear God's life within them — that is the life that constantly rebuilds them. We are made to bear Christ, to be like Mary. Beginning from any other standpoint will miss the mark. Perhaps this is why the relationship between Saint Francis and Saint Clare was so special. They both understood the importance of following the steps of Jesus as Mary did. Clare desired to be like Francis because Francis was like Jesus. While Francis was repairing the physical building of San Damiano, he said, "Come and help me in the work of the church of San Damiano which, in the future, will be a monastery of ladies through whose fame and life our heavenly Father will be glorified throughout the church."[21]

Roughly six years later, his vision came true when Saint Clare and her sisters made this the home base of their order. "Clare," says Father Benedict, "did not start out to be a reformer but intended to respond to the call to love God and give herself personally to Christ. The same call had been received by Saint Francis."[22] Francis, Clare, and all friars living as they did were, first and foremost, living a life that showed their desire to lay down their whole selves out of humility, sacrifice, and service like Christ. They knew that doing so would make them like him, and being like him would bring them closer to Jesus. That is all that matters. Then as now, personal faith was the antidote to a broken time.

Following the demands of Christ is no small task. Jesus does not force anyone to be with him, but those who wish to follow him must make him their everything. We must decide whether we are giving him everything or not. Many believe that if we lighten up the demands of Jesus and become less strict, then more people will see the love and beauty that the Church has to offer. Some would even claim that Saint Francis proposed this style of renewal. On the contrary, Francis was intense. He required his followers to give absolutely everything to Christ

— physical possessions, wealth, titles, everything. Francis renounced everything when he accepted Jesus' call. He required this of his followers as well. Every single belonging would have to be given up when a man entered the order. He could never accept money again. Upon entering, each man would be given two tunics for the entire year.[23]

His way of life was and is demanding because Jesus asked a lot of his followers. In fact, he commanded everything from them: wives, families, careers, and the stability that this world offers. Jesus demands everything of us, too. Yet this truth is the most forgotten aspect of what it means to be a true follower of Jesus. Handing Christ our entire selves is not the end goal but the beginning of the rebuilding process.

Christ demands these things of us because he wants to purify us and make us like God. The demands of a relationship with him mean that we will fall short, and that's normal. The truth of the matter is: "Any relationship with the living God always leads to tension, conflict and failure and then to repentance and to reform. From repentance and reform, starting over again, comes a rebirth to holiness and renewal."[24] Father Benedict's words here ring true as we consider the very story of salvation. It begins with the tension and conflict of Adam and Eve's sin. The consequence of their sin leads to a plethora of failures throughout the history of Israel. All the while, God is calling his people back to himself. All they have to do is cling to his love and give him permission to upend their lives. Repentance is that simple.

When John the Baptist arrived on the scene, he called people to change their ways. Later, Jesus began his ministry with the same message, because repentance is the first necessary step. Calvary and the empty tomb were the divine moments that made our relationship with God right again. Coming into contact with these realities was what spurred on the apostles and early disciples to needed repentance and reform of their own hearts. If we want to grow in holiness, we can look to these moments and allow their power to conquer our hearts, too. Jesus' own sacrificial love is what ultimately reformed the life of the apostles, and that experience leapt exponentially into the renewal and holiness of the life of the early Church.

Today we face a multitude of challenges in the Church and in the world. The very magnitude of the issues at hand shows that seeking personal renewal in the spirit of Saint Francis is the way forward. "The diseases," Father Benedict notes, "of materialism, selfism, cynicism and religious skepticism are so widespread and acute in our society and so pervasive in our culture that I do not believe there is any way other than personal conversion to work toward the reform of the renewal."[25] God in his wisdom knew that salvation would come about through the birth, action, death, and resurrection of one person: Jesus Christ. Salvation was brought about through an individual. One person can truly change the world.

Father Groeschel continues his explanation: "Mother Teresa once confided to me that if she had not picked up the first homeless man in Calcutta four decades ago, she would never have been able to help hundreds of thousands who are dependent on her and her sisters and brothers today. We have to start and keep going. We cannot all be Mother Teresa, but we can be who we are supposed to be."[26]

These insights from Father Benedict and Mother Teresa come centuries after Saint Francis, but they portray what he knew to be most true. Francis was simply fascinated by becoming like Christ. He took ownership of the fact that this meant he would need to be continuously repaired himself, even as he tried to rebuild the Church. When that is the mode of our every movement, then we will light the world on fire around us as we begin lifting up those in need.

Reforming the Renewal

Later in life Francis often found the opportunity to correct his brothers. He did so as a gentle father, and he did so always out of a desire to form holiness, not tear down weakness. This is what I experienced in my own brokenness, as I shared in the introduction. The forgiveness of my wife was not an acceptance of my flaws but a call to change my ways. It was an experience of gospel repentance because I was being invited to something more — something difficult but good for me.

One Easter Sunday, Francis learned that a friary was making use of fine tablecloths, linens, silverware, and glasses. So he disguised himself and knocked on the door of the friary. He held out a bowl and was given a piece of bread. He continued to sit on the ground by the fire. He then spoke for the entire room to hear and said, "Since your table is too fancy for the poor who go begging at people's doors and who, more than other religious, are bound to imitate the Savior's humility, permit me to sit here, like a real Friar Minor."[27]

If becoming like Christ means that we must constantly be turning away from sin and toward repentance, then what does this look like and how is it accomplished? How can imperfect people like us change the world? First, we must note that this is not a task to "accomplish" but a desire in the heart to live by. We are not trying to simply check the box of being a good Catholic. The infinite hole in our heart can only be filled by the infinite One. That is why we move toward repentance, recognizing our need — that we are creatures and not gods. We have a Creator-Father who is constantly pursuing our hearts, even as we go about our business, not really paying much attention to him.

This provides a gut check opportunity for each of us. If you are reading this book, it is most likely because you desire to change the tides of the times and because you seek deeper intimacy with God. You see that there is brokenness out there and that our world needs God. Reforming the renewal means that we first admit that we need to repair our own rundown hearts before anything else.

The whole process really begins with the way that we view sin and the way that we see ourselves. Any movement toward the glorification of self and away from the need of a good Father leads us into sin, period. Both Saint Francis and Father Benedict had a keen awareness of their own inadequacy. This was not a mechanism that made them beat themselves down into loathing, but an awareness that holiness means continually repenting. It means that our heart lives in the repair shop of grace. All disciples should cultivate in their hearts a focus on continual conversion.

Father Benedict wrote that it is "clear that reform, the positive effort to change and overcome our tendency toward evil, is the cutting edge of an integrated Christian life. Those who pretend that the community of followers of Christ is perfect have neglected to take into account this important fact of life."[28] Those who run to Christ and fall at his feet are the self-proclaimed sinners of the world. They do not, however, promote themselves as sinners in order to appear righteous. They do so because they are on the path to living in the truth and in the liberation from sin that only Christ can bring.

Father Benedict also quotes Pope St. John Paul II, who wrote that "being converted means continually giving an account before the Lord of our hearts about our service, our zeal, our fidelity … of our negligences and sins, of our timidity, our lack of faith and hope, of our thinking only 'in a human way' and not 'in a divine way.'"[29] When we give that honest account to God after serious reflection and deliberation, we see that conversion is what we are always in need of. (We will dive into this "giving an account" more when we discuss the daily examination of conscience in the next chapter.)

The following words are written by Father Benedict and are inspired by Sacred Scripture, but they personify what Saint Francis knew with every ounce of his heart:

> The word renewal ... is a good word. In the Pauline con-
> text it means to return to the *power* of the Holy Spirit
> and let Him *make us new again* (Rom 12:2). But before
> renewal can occur, reform is necessary. True spiritual re-
> newal is not simply cultural or educational. It is not sim-
> ply restating truths to make them more compatible with
> a new age. True renewal is above all *a return* to God. It
> is a *daily, ongoing* repentance, an attempt to accept the
> Good News in all its unthinkable and incomprehensible
> grandeur and to pick oneself up and try to respond to
> that call. Renewal without reform is spiritually devas-
> tating.[30]

Disciples allow the power of God's breath to work through them constantly. This is embodied by a daily return to Jesus' actions and words and presence. Every day we begin anew by accepting the invitation to live out the radical demands of the Christian life, because love commands us to respond with everything that we are. Only from this foundation will conversion and then renewal arise. His breath must serve as the spark; our daily commitment to repentance must be the tool we use to begin.

Reform and Renewal in the Church

We know what is needed from the individual in order for us to renew the earth: We must constantly repent and draw close to Christ. We also know that we do not repent merely so that we can become advocates for social change, but so that we can become holy by being united to the Son of God. Communion is the primary goal — not because we want to be viewed as holy, but because we desire him. Being with Jesus and becoming like him is all that matters. Holiness, though, will radically impact whatever it touches, so renewal will be inevitable.

Holy contact brings about change. This is the spiritual logic behind many of Jesus' healings. Blood is dried up when it touches his tassel (see Lk 8:44). Leprosy is driven out by his touch (Mt 8:3). Even death is conquered by his hand making contact with Jairus's daughter (Mk 5:41–42). Saint Francis brought this divine logic to life. His commitment to personal faith in Jesus allowed him to make contact with the Son of God in such a way that it healed and transformed him. Then Jesus used Francis as a conduit to transform and heal others.

Every member of the Christian faithful is asked to consider how they are doing on their path to what we might call "Christification." We are not looking for abstract piety, but earth-trodden holiness that has one's feet on the ground and one's heart united to the Triune God who is love, who is relationship. As individual members of the Church, we must be uniform in how we present the gospel message because it is the person of Jesus Christ that is at stake when we proclaim it. Yes, this concerns the clergy, but it is also the primary task of the lay faithful. The entire Body of Christ must preach his name. We cannot have Jesus' message be spoken only from the pulpit on Sundays or only from someone who has a microphone and works for our parish. His merciful love and the fire of his heart must be lived and shared in everyday experiences that stretch from our beings naturally.

The manner in which families speak about and practice their faith is the number one most important factor for what faith in the Church will look like in the next generation. The family is the place where children first learn how to be good. The family is where children see, or don't see, the importance of prayer and worship. The family is where they will experience what true, sacrificial love is.

All these areas will provide the soil that will allow children to grow up and raise their own families to be practicing Catholics. They will ultimately have to make their own decision about the Faith; there is no guarantee. But how they experience the vitality of faith in their developmental years will strongly determine whether or not they will be open to a vocation as a priest or religious. Simply put, if following Jesus is not the most important thing for a family, if the Faith is not intentionally and intensely lived, then it will not be the most important thing for the child when he or she grows up.

Deep down, all children and young adults desire to be challenged by the crazy nature of sacrificial love. That is why we must present the Faith as something that requires much of us, because in reality, it requires everything. An analogy can be applied to the state of vocations to the priesthood in America. When speaking about the rapid decline of vocations to the priesthood and religious life, Father Benedict highlighted the inherent issue at large: "Whereas the French Revolution and the waves of persecution that followed it occasioned a huge number of priestly and religious vocations and an unparalleled missionary outreach, the skepticism and religious cynicism of the 1960s and 1970s have had the opposite effect in America and much of Europe."[31]

The rate at which Catholics accept the call to be priests or religious brothers or sisters is not the only measurement of a flourishing faith, but it is a critical one. These are men and women who have decided, against all mockery and defamation by the culture, to give their entire lives to Jesus Christ. They have heard cries from the society that Christ was only a man and that his writings are all fables. They have heard the accusations against celibacy and have been encouraged to desire for unhindered materialism and wealth. And yet, they pour themselves out anyway. They lie prostrate on the marble floors of cathedrals, and they profess their lives in small monasteries and friaries around the world because they know that it is their relationship with Jesus Christ that outweighs any odds or attacks. That outlandish, reckless love is what they know they are called to.

So, yes, the decline in vocations is a cause for pause and deliberation. But it is also a sign that there are not enough families living out the truth of Jesus' mission and message. All religious brothers, sisters, and priests originally come from a family. Those families are first made up of individual spouses who are asked to consider the call of Christ each day. That is why the focus on repentance, humility, and Christ leads to so much renewal: The conversion of one individual has the capacity to impact everyone in the next generation of a household.

People will only find the call of Christ compelling if it is handed on as he intended. Jesus calls us to leave everything behind and follow him — not because he is needy but because the things we cling to only mask our desire for him. Jesus never turned people away who wished to follow him, but he always clarified for them what it meant to follow him. He allowed the rich young man to leave when he was unwilling to sell everything (see Lk 18:23). Christ did not make exceptions for the rich man, nor does he make them for us. He allowed the crowds to leave after he told them that they must eat his flesh (Jn 6:66). Jesus did not cover up the truth for them so that he could sound accepting or loving. Only when the gospel message is proclaimed with clarity and accepted in its radical nature do people experience a transformation.

Promoting a faith that does not really demand much from the individual leads to a dead religion. Christians cannot modify teaching or make exceptions for Jesus' tough commands. We cannot waiver before a culture that calls us bigots. We also cannot run from a culture that appears to have no place for us. Watering down the Faith and proposing a relationship with Jesus that is not radical only deadens the Faith. Any time there has been a true reform of life that led to renewal, it was caused by a call to discipleship that remained true to what Jesus actually asked of his followers. Francis knew this, and it was exactly why he was so successful in gaining followers. Staying true to Jesus is the call, and then Christ will take care of the rest. Doing our part means that we trust him and assent to his word.

Fleeing from Christ leaves us empty. Divorcing the words and demands of Jesus from his meaning and intention only leads to a faith that is less likely to be believed (which makes sense, because it is literally the wrong belief). However, we do not want to give people the ultimatum to simply become like us or be left behind. "If we attempt reform without repentance, it becomes self-righteousness and bitter zeal."[32] Renewal takes time and patience. Changing one's life is an offer of grace that comes from God who counts on human vessels to walk with others in their trials, not desert them when they need us the most.

Therefore, the way of Saint Francis is modeled on the mission of Christ. Francis desired to live a different life than the earlier monastics, whose life was built on stability. A monk lived in a certain place for the rest of his life, and his life was scheduled meticulously around service and prayer. This type of life was built on the early Church that we see described in the second chapter of the Acts of the Apostles: "They devoted themselves to the teaching of the apostles and to the communal life, to the breaking of the bread and to the prayers. All who believed were together and had all things in common" (Acts 2:42, 44). This is how monastics seek holiness of life. Francis, however, saw that Christ was calling him to establish a different way.

Saint Francis's way of life was not built on the early Church, but on the public ministry of Jesus as he walked the earth. Francis was not completely original in this idea, but his way of life was different from anything that had come before, because he followed the Catholic Church with unreserved obedience. He believed that the ideal way of life was the way that Jesus lived and acted with his apostles during his earthly ministry. They lived together and moved about from place to place, ministering to those who needed aid. They lived a life of poverty that depended on the goodness of others for their next meal or place of rest, and they endured the suffering that resulted from that life.

Many would probably argue that the life of a follower of Francis is too difficult, too extreme. Surely God does not desire for us to have such difficulties; he wants us to be happy. It's important to understand that the sacrifices and sufferings are not ends in themselves. The disciple does not grasp at suffering for suffering's sake but seeks to follow the same pathway that Jesus took to the Father. That is why Saint Francis would often describe his way of life as walking in the footprints of Jesus. Jesus' road to saving the world was offering his very being to God the Father. Since he calls us to be one with him, we must also offer ourselves as a sacrificial oblation. The repair mission of Saint Francis requires this way of life only because that is what Jesus asks of us.

The arenas of culture, government, and Church are all necessary to engage in if we wish to bring about renewal. The fight, however, is not one that is entered into with a desire to harm, but to restore. We should view our role as healers or medics on the front lines.

Reflect

- What quality of Saint Francis stands out to you the most? Why?
- In what specific ways do you think you are being invited to deeper conversion right now?
- How is Jesus calling you right now to live more in his footprints?

3
Beginning the Process
of Rebuilding

The spiritual is the practical. When Saint Francis heard the call to rebuild the Church, he first began by repairing what he could see: the decrepit church buildings in his own town. God had more in mind for Francis, but his first instinct was not far off. The practical things around us that are in need of repair are the perfect place for us to begin to allow renewal to take shape.

Ultimately, Saint Francis shows the world that we are best able to rebuild the brokenness that surrounds us when we move from the foundation of Christ's gaze. Those piercing but loving eyes of Christ enabled Francis to believe what was being asked of him, and they drove him to serve the lost, the least, and the forgotten in Assisi and beyond. The only way that we can restore our age is by moving from that same starting point: the way that Jesus looks at us.

The shared mission of every single person is life-altering union with the living God. The particular manner in which that is lived out depends on our gifts and circumstances. The beauty and power of the Christian Faith is that everyone's mission is fundamentally the same. There is a love story whose vigor runs unleashed through our veins. Yet we convince ourselves that we are small and insignificant in the grand scheme of things. We convince ourselves that there's nothing all that special about who we are. We are just another person of the nearly eight billion on earth. We grew up as normal individuals, we went to school, we tried our best, we got a job, and now we are where we are.

This normalizing of our dignity and mission drives our Father crazy. In order to break this mindset, Jesus comes to look us in the eyes and call us to something great and unrepeatable — like he did for Francis. There is no one else on the planet who can accomplish the task that he has set before you. The only way to find out this mission is to look at him and allow him to see you.

A look can change everything. Princeton psychologists discovered that it takes only a tenth of a second for people to form first impressions of others.[1] They also found that first impressions are very difficult to alter once they have been formulated. When we get a glimpse of the way someone appears, primarily how they look at us, we can gauge something powerful about their identity.

A gaze is powerful among human beings, but it is supernatural between God and man. When Jesus looked at people, he saw them through and through. His words come with a message, but the way he looks at his brothers and sisters is the starting point. The message that Francis received to repair the Church and change his life was placed in words, but its context was the gaze of Jesus from the cross of San Damiano.

Any chance we have to repair our own heart, our own family, our own parish, and the Church will begin with this look. It is the gaze of God made man that will restore and rebuild. This is not a pious platitude, but immovable truth and power. Once Francis met Christ as a real person, he could not get that gaze out of his head. He was infatuated with Jesus because he saw in his eyes the answer to everything that he ever wanted. He saw the man that he was made to be.

Renewal began with Francis — and will begin in our lives — with a look.

The Varanasi Letter

How do we catch the gaze of Christ?

On a retreat in my first years after college, I encountered a message that changed my life. Fr. Michael Gaitley, a priest of the Congregation of Marian Fathers of the Immaculate Conception and author of *33 Days to Morning Glory*, led the retreat. His sessions and message revolved around a new book idea he had that became known as *The Second Greatest Story Ever Told*. This was the story of the desire for God's mercy to reign powerfully across the world.

In one of Father Gaitley's sessions he spoke about Mother Teresa. Specifically, he highlighted the little-known words of a letter she wrote to her community in the final years of her life. The letter became known as the Varanasi Letter. Father Gaitley used the words from this letter to showcase what it means to encounter Jesus face-to-face.

Here is the portion of her letter that he focused on:

> Do you really know the living Jesus — not from books, but from being with Him in your heart? Have you heard the loving words He speaks to you? … Never give up on this daily intimate contact with Jesus as a real living person — not just an idea.
>
> How can we last even one day living our life without hearing Jesus say "I love you?" — impossible. Our soul

needs that as much as the body needs to breathe the air. If not, prayer is dead — meditation is only thinking. Jesus wants you each to hear Him — speaking in the silence of your heart. ... Not only He loves you, even more — He longs for you. He misses you when you don't come close. He thirsts for you.

He loves you always, even when you don't feel worthy. Even if you are not accepted by others, even by yourself sometimes — He is the one who always accepts you. ... Why does Jesus say "I Thirst?" What does it mean? Something so hard to explain in words — if you remember anything from Mother's letter, remember this — "I Thirst" is something much deeper than just Jesus saying "I Love you."

Until you know deep inside that Jesus thirsts for you — you can't begin to know who He wants to be for you. Or who He wants you to be. ... He knows your weakness, He wants only your love, wants only the chance to love you.[2]

The invitation on this retreat was to take the words of Mother's letter and sit with them — to pray with them like our life depended on them. I took the invite seriously, and it changed my life. I had spent a good portion of my college life in prayer before the Blessed Sacrament and praying the Rosary. I had never missed a Sunday Mass in my life, but this altered everything.

For the first time in my life, I actually met Jesus through these words. He was no longer an idea. Being Catholic was no longer the equivalent of being a part of a club or a team. I knew that the Catholic Faith was meant to be a radical and intimate relationship with the God of the universe, and now I experienced him as a real living person. In a profound way, I encountered Christ.

This happened because I could see the way that Christ looked at me through the holiness and insights of Mother Teresa. I realized that his gaze is always directed toward me. On this day it became more real than ever. As I write these words, nine years later, I can say that I have recited the words of the Varanasi Letter almost every day since — not out of obligation, but out of a desire to continue to encounter Jesus' gaze every single day.

In a very, very small way, I think this must have been what Francis experienced. His invitation to rebuild the Church of Christ came with a look from Jesus as he hung on the cross in that small church building. The look of Christ changed his life, and that same look is what the saints experienced daily. That did not mean that they felt warm and fuzzy every day they woke up sacrificing for the Lord, but it did mean that they knew what their foundation was.

If we desire to begin to rebuild the world around us, we must begin from the same starting point as the other rebuilders who came before us: intimacy with Jesus as a real, living person.

The Idea Versus the Truth

Every single person on the planet is in need of healing and renewal. We all need deeper conversion and commitment to Christ. This is not one idea among many in Christianity. This is the deepest truth of Jesus' preaching and of the life of a disciple. Do your ideas about the Faith align with this reality?

If you are like me, this was not something that was radically evident to you your entire life. Most of my life I was sure of the fact that Catholicism was about following rules and showing up to Sunday Mass. Of course, we are called to be nice and kind to others, but there was no specific way of accomplishing that, in my mind. I have found that nothing could be further from the truth. With Saint Francis, we view a specific way to live out the Gospel. His way is not one among many ideas about how to be a disciple; rather, his way arrives at the heart of the matter.

Whatever ideas we might have about being Christian, what if we placed them to the side and began to live more like Saint Francis? What if we could annihilate the "idea" of being faithful and instead live in the truth of following Jesus?

Francis was able to bear tremendous fruit in the lives of his contemporaries because he could see the individual heart behind the sin or false idea about God and reality. Francis was "the proclaimer of evangelical perfection and began publicly to preach penance with simplicity. Moreover, his statements ... penetrated the marrow of the heart and provided stunned amazement in those who heard them."[3] Faith wasn't an idea to him. We know that people have wrong ideas about who God is or what life is about. Rational dialogue and debate are critical, but we can only arrive at a place to converse with another person after we have spent time loving him or her. That will be the soil for any fruitful conversion to occur.

Relationships are the only starting point for repairing and renewing. "Relational ministry" is a popular term when it comes to ministering to the youth in the Church. The idea is that you spend time simply getting to know young people before you sit them down and open up the Bible or dissect the arguments for and against Church doctrine. People are not arguments to be won, but individuals to be encountered. Only once a level of trust has been established can there be any fruitful transition to speaking about the Faith.

Jesus spent time with people, and he never viewed them as "projects." As mentioned in chapter 2, the Greek word *therapeuo* is often used in Scripture when Jesus heals someone. This word communicates the fact that Jesus spent intentional time with the person and did not simply snap his fingers. He can heal quickly, and he does so at times, but he also makes special note that healing comes from spending time with him.

To begin the process of rebuilding our own hearts, we must first spend time with Jesus — a lot of time. We must be people who live from prayer and spend a significant amount of time in prayer each day. Prayer must be something that we do, not something that we just talk about or reference. Prayer is not about what we are reading or what we do in our time of meditation. Prayer must be intimacy with the Lord.

Second, if we desire to bring healing and renewal, we must be willing to spend time with those we want to heal. Whether it is family members, friends, coworkers, or acquaintances, we must show patience and build our relationship with them first. From there we will see that the possibilities to inject the truth in our conversations will become endless, because it will no longer be solely about the ideas we know are true, but rather about a person we love.

Deeper conversion only comes about when faith becomes personal. We must be authentic and not simply spew nice ideas. Our evangelization only comes across as real if we speak to God each day as if he were a person sitting next to us. Make constant contact with the Lord. He is not an imaginary friend but he who is Being itself. The time we carve out for prayer, even if that prayer is "God, I don't know if you're really there. Reveal yourself to me if you are," will bear fruit beyond our imagining.

Jesus frequently went off to pray on his own for this reason. He desired to be alone with the Father and to have the space to be completely honest with him. The testimony of Saint Francis's life is that the Father in heaven always takes care of us and comes to our side. So that is the message we must count on and the one we must deliver. This is the truth of our faith.

Like Francis, make faith real through constant conversation with Jesus as a real living person, not an idea. People do not change their lives for ideas or philosophies, but we will change our lives for our friends and loved ones. In order to rebuild our

culture and Church, we must be reliant on personal faith —
which is the only faith for a Christian.

True Devotion Is a Commitment to Prayer

Following the way of Francis and Jesus means that we love
Christ, and we allow that love to flow into our daily interactions
with others. This begins with a promise.

We make a promise despite not knowing what our circumstances might be in the future when we are called to keep that
promise. Something might come up that makes keeping our
promise more difficult, or something might occur that appears
to be more important than keeping our promise — but if we are
men and women of our word, we will keep to our promise, no
matter the circumstances.

Once Saint Francis encountered Jesus and saw the way the
Son of God looked at him, he knew that he was called to devote
his entire life to Christ. Leaving his wealth and family made it
easier for him to commit to a life of prayer, but as he became
more well known, his schedule filled up immensely. This meant
that he had to find time for intimate prayer, and he had to choose
what he would *not* commit to in order to pray each day. The
same is true for you and for me.

Whether we are single, or husbands and wives, mothers and
fathers, or priests and religious, we are called to have a consistent and powerful prayer life. This cannot happen if we plan
our prayer around all the "more important things" that we have
going on. Prayer must take precedence over our calendars. We
must schedule concrete time to pray every single day, or we will
easily fall into the trap of deciding to be productive over being
prayerful.

Due to the busy nature of most people's lives, this will mean
that we must make a firm and important promise to God that we
will pray at a specific time of day and for a specific duration of

time every day. This comes from the wisdom of Christ and the practical prudence of religious life. Jesus was among the crowds and his disciples constantly. However, there are many moments when we read that he went off to the mountain to pray or that he went off on his own in order to spend time with his Father (see Mt 14:23; Mk 6:46–47; Jn 6:15). If Jesus found this to be essential to his ministry, then we must make it a non-negotiable of our existence as well.

Francis made a firm commitment to pray every single day — no exceptions. He demanded the same of his brothers. Laypeople who live and work in the world cannot abide by the same prayer schedule, but we can learn from the way Francis and the members of his order today schedule their prayer time.

Practically speaking, this will mean waking up early rather than staying up late. At the end of a day, we are filled with exhaustion, and our minds can be racing, thinking about all that has happened. We are also more in control of when we wake up. To make this work, though, we must be committed to going to sleep at a reasonable hour. Waking up early is a sacrifice, but when we make the promise to arise when our alarm goes off and give that time over to God, the rewards are immeasurable. If waking up is a real struggle for you, offer your tiredness for your spouse and kids or the conversion of someone you love.

Allow God to own the first part of your day. Make the promise that you will give this time over to him.

Anything that is holy is dedicated to God for his use. The intimacy that Francis had with Christ, receiving his loving gaze, was only possible because he made the commitment to be in the presence of God each day for a lengthy period of time. In order to be equipped for renewal, we must do the same. This cannot be an empty promise. Prayer cannot be the last item on our to-do list. Marking the beginning of the day for God means that we give him our first fruits; then the rest of the day can be entered into with him in mind.

Truly entering into that time of prayer is an entirely different story, and it is a lifelong process. The goal of all prayer should always be intimacy. We must avoid checking the boxes in prayer and being satisfied with the time spent with him over the heart-to-heart that we enter into during that time. Routine is important, but at the same time, the process can never become the goal. An important question to ask about our prayer life is: What does my prayer do to me? Is there transformation that occurs as a result of my prayer, or is it simply about feeling better that I have kept my commitment to wake up and give over a certain amount of time in union with God?

Have you ever been in conversation with a friend or family member and at some point during the back and forth realize that you have not been paying close attention to what they have been saying? Maybe you neglected to hear an important detail of a story, so you are lost. Maybe you missed the name of a person in the story, so you are not exactly sure who your friend or family member is talking about. Our minds can tend to drift away from who or what is in front of us and become more concerned with things of the past or possibilities in the future.

Prayer can often become like that. We might go a lengthy period of time in prayer and then realize that we have been spending the majority of our attention on something other than God. If you are reading this book, you are probably someone who does pray and who desires to grow deeper in relationship with Christ. Something has happened in your life and heart that is drawing you to God. That is exactly what happened to Saint Francis. You probably did not have Jesus speak to you from a crucifix in a deserted chapel in Italy, but something has happened to you.

Like Francis, we must remember that we have been called. We have been invited into an epic journey that invites us to hand over our entire hearts to Christ. Nothing less will do. So when we pray, that is what our God is asking us for: our heart and our entire selves.

Consider this question: If Jesus did not have the perfect knowledge of God (if he did not know everything about you already), how much would he know about you solely based on what you have shared with him? Do you share your heart with him? Do you talk to Christ about your hurts and desires and fears and greatest joys? These are the conversations that he would have had with his disciples as they journeyed for three years ministering together. These are the discussions he longs to have with you as well.

All these questions and considerations are healthy, and they must be asked. However, they can never be asked if we do not first commit to the daily promise to hand over to God a significant part of our day so we can encounter him, experience him, and see the way he looks at us. Only that will allow us to become changed and to begin the process of rebuilding and restoring.

Consider Your Deathbed

Modern men and women rarely pause or retreat from ordinary life. We can often neglect to slow down and reflect on what is most important. The forces of sin, evil, and our own laziness can easily drown out the fact that this life is not all there is.

Prayer and silence will be our best modes forward to begin to rebuild ourselves and the world. We are not simply speaking of formal prayer time, but of the conscious awareness that Jesus is with us in everything we do. Prayer, at its best, is the abiding awareness of Christ being at our side.

The world might think this is wasted time and not practical to address the mess we experience in our families, in our country, and in our own hearts. As we will see, Francis knew the interior life was the answer to the repair project of the Church. Each of us has flaws and sins that we know are rooted deep within our habits and being. Retreating into prayer, stepping away from the world to be present to him, allows Jesus to gently and lovingly tear these things out of our lives so we can better know who we were made to be.

You — the ordinary man or woman reading these words in your seemingly mundane bedroom or on the train car to work — you are the one who will change the tide. You are the one God is calling to rebuild his world. The genesis of this movement is in turning inward, intentionally retreating each day to pray even if others might think you are crazy or wasting your time.

This tactic works in the military battlefield, but it is also applicable in the battlefield for the human soul. In the film *Braveheart*, Mel Gibson plays the historical character of William Wallace, a great Scottish warrior who aided the fight against the English. In one scene, Wallace arrives on the battlefield to see that the Scottish are heavily outnumbered. Some soldiers are beginning to flee before the battle even begins. The cowardice of his army leads Wallace to deliver a speech that has become famous in the world of cinema.

Wallace declares to the entire army: "I see a whole army of my countrymen here in defiance of tyranny. You have come to fight as free men, and free men you are. What would you do with that freedom? Will you fight?" Several veteran soldiers respond that they will not fight. They will run, and they will live.

Wallace replies: "Aye, fight and you may die. Run, and you'll live — at least a while. And dying in your beds many years from now, would you be willing to trade all the days from this day to that for one chance, just one chance to come back here and tell our enemies that they may take our lives, but they'll never take our freedom!" The army erupts in cheers and prepares for battle. Many died that day, but the victory was theirs.

To convince the Scots to fight the battle Wallace employs the image of their deathbed. If they flee the battlefield they will live "a while." Everyone dies eventually. The question is not *if* you are going to die, but how are you going to spend your life before death comes. They have the chance to lay it all on the line for freedom and for their country. Giving up in the face of that chance will only lead to regret because they are rejecting an opportunity to be heroic.

As Catholics, we must always be cognizant of our deathbed. We are asked to live from a deathbed mentality. The major symbol of our faith highlights this fact: The cross is the most famous ancient tool to inflict pain, suffering, and death on criminals. Yet the cross is raised as the emblem of the Christian Faith, making it clear that God wants us to contemplate our death on a daily basis. Considering one's deathbed is necessary so we will live with the vigor that this life deserves.

Martin Luther King Jr. once said, "If a man has not discovered something that he will die for, he isn't fit to live." What are the things and people that we would make the ultimate sacrifice for? Who resides at the center of our lives? We do not need to be heroes on a battlefield to change someone's life forever. All it takes is a resolution to accept the call to repair what has been given to each of us from our baptism.

Jesus Christ was born so he could offer his life for the salvation of the world. We also are called to live our lives in sacrifice and service to a cause greater than ourselves. Practically speaking, we can sacrifice for others by praying and fasting for the deeper conversion of our loved ones, friends, and those with whom we work. We can offer our suffering, with our death in mind, for someone else who is experiencing physical or emotional pain.

Considering our deathbed can also make us more willing to sacrifice our name and reputation, by a willingness to speak about the Faith in spaces that scare us. Maybe there is someone at work with whom you feel called to share the Faith, but you are afraid of what they might say. Maybe there are times when you could have spoken about the Faith to a loved one, but you put it off because you feared they might consider you judgmental.

Meditating on the suffering of Christ and on our own deathbed can bring greater clarity for the need to act on our faith in a public and powerful way. Doing so will, most likely, come at a cost. Jesus promised that it would be difficult to follow him. However, if we do so in a humble way and from a place of prayer, we will be like Saint Francis — and the impact will be surprising.

If we reflect on our deathbed before committing to act, we will inevitably become men and women who commit to the good. Francis knew that Christ laid his life on the line for him, and this moved him to sacrifice each day with his own death in mind. This did not lead to morbidity but to heroism and radical trust. For this reason, Francis would reference the end of life as "Sister Death." Regularly contemplating this sibling of humanity helps us to remember our neighbor and our God. The deathbed mentality fosters a heart that knows that the best thing we can do is surrender our heart to Christ as Francis did.

Walk Humbly with Our God

When speaking to a bishop on one occasion, Saint Francis said: "My Lord, my brothers are called 'lesser' precisely so they do not presume to become 'greater.' They have been called this to teach them to stay down to earth, and to follow the footprints of Christ's humility, which in the end will exalt them above others in the sight of the saints."[4]

Francis loved humility because this was the mode of God's interaction with humanity. The God of the universe became man — a man born of poor carpenters from the middle of nowhere. Because of this, we can literally place our feet in the same spot as Christ's feet. Humility comes from the Latin word *hu-*

militas, which means "that earth which is beneath us." Christian humility is concerned with the acknowledgment that everything we are and can do is dependent on God, not ourselves. It is not a negative view of human beings but a radical dependence on God based on who he is.

Humility is how we walk and live like God. The entire nature of the Trinity is to live for the Other, and so to be self-centered and selfish is to act opposite to who God is. We see this in Jesus' interactions with his disciples as well as in the last few days of his life. The emptying forth of his energy and life for others defined him. The God of the universe became the servant of all.

This is how we are called to live. This does not mean we should become a doormat. Humility is about sacrificial love. There are so many ways that we can begin to walk humbly with Christ and with Saint Francis. Some of these might sound childish or naïve, but they are truly rooted in the life and witness of Francis. Humility does not come easy, because we are too often inclined to make ourselves the center of attention. Yet it is the school we must enter if we want to grow in holiness. How do we do this?

First, "Praise God!" If you meet any of the CFRs today, you might hear them speaking these words. Like Saint Francis, the friars constantly give thanks to God for all the gifts they receive. Ultimately, everything comes from God, and we are always invited to show him gratitude for the good things he has given us.

Consider how often you voice your gratitude to God in your own personal prayer. Do you intentionally give him thanks for your job, your family, your health, or other good things you have in your life? If you do, how often do you do so? Francis was known to give praise to God every single day for everything, even things that seemed insignificant — the weather, the sun, the moon, his brothers and sisters, his food, and his way of life. Francis was grateful even though he had so little.

When gratitude is our foundation, we recognize that all things comes from our Father, who desires to take care of us. Just as a small child is taught to say "thank you," so we must learn to give consistent thanks to God each and every day. This breeds humility because we see that we are not responsible for the good things we have.

Second, make conversations about the other person. The Gospels record 183 questions Jesus was asked by others. Yet only on three of those occasions does he give a direct answer. Most of the time he answers a question with another question. There are many reasons why he might have chosen to do so, but perhaps most importantly, this allows him to build a relationship with the other person so their interaction is not simply a transaction of information but an encounter.

Another effect of asking questions is that you make the conversation about the other person. Jesus had infinite wisdom. The thousands who heard him preach could testify to this. The way he spoke literally transformed hearts and lives. In the majority of conversations, however, he did not deem it necessary to throw down all of the knowledge he had. He wanted the people with whom he spoke to know that he cared for them and he loved them.

When we speak to people, are we mostly talking about ourselves, or are we interested in what is going on in the life of the other person? Are we more invested in getting our opinion across or do we actually desire to get to know the other person, even if that will make it more difficult or require more patience from us?

Let us take a lesson from Christ: Make conversations about the other person. Thoughtful listening is key. We should always consider how much we speak over how much we listen. We should also reflect on how attentive we are to others when we are listening. Thoughtful listening leaves the space open to absorb what the other person needs and how we can show love to them. This means that we must pray for the humility to care more about the other than about ourselves and our own initiatives. This does not mean we never speak or that we simply pepper others with a million questions. Use your discernment to carefully think about how much you talk about yourself over the other person. Make a commitment to give the spotlight over to the other person more often.

Another great way to foster humility and become rebuilt by becoming more like Christ is to choose the lower task or option more often. We do not want to get in the habit of denying ourselves of good things just because we want to deny ourselves. However, there is tremendous wisdom in sacrificing something good that we could have had in order to attach ourselves more to the humble and sacrificial nature of Christ.

This can be done by eating less than you might prefer, volunteering to do the house chore that no one else wants to do, or even by being willing to take the late hour feeding of your infant so your spouse does not have to. When we choose the way that is not what we expected or the route that requires more sacrifice, we become like Christ. We do not simply play a copycat game, though. Being rooted in humility makes us more human because we recognize that we depend on God for everything. When we depend more on him, God makes us more alive than we ever have been.

Keep the Stigmata at Your Side

In the Office of Readings for the feast day of St. John of the Cross, we read an excerpt from one of his Spiritual Canticles. At face value one portion of the reading is puzzling, but it becomes clearer when we read it in the light of Saint Francis and other saints: "For this reason the apostle Paul said of Christ: In him are hidden all the treasures of the wisdom and knowledge of God.

The soul cannot enter into these treasures, nor attain them, unless it first crosses into and enters the thicket of suffering, enduring interior and exterior labors, and unless it first receives from God very many blessings in the intellect and in the senses, and has undergone long spiritual training."

Directly before Abraham is about to take the life of Isaac, an angel is sent by God and prevents him from doing so. We are then told that he saw a ram caught in a thicket (see Gn 22:13). Rams are massive animals with immense physical strength, yet this one was stuck with no way out of the tangle of brush.

You have probably experienced something like this in your own life — a season when the pain or suffering of your experience seemed insurmountable and paralyzing. John of the Cross, Francis of Assisi, and all the saints knew these seasons of life as well. Francis fasted and lived in challenging circumstances for decades. He made commitments to sacrifice for God and others that impacted his health in many ways.

We also know that he received the wounds of Christ (the stigmata) later in his life, and that this brought him tremendous anguish. Francis lived a holy life for years prior to this and had countless spiritual experiences that left him in ecstasy. He was in union with God in his daily prayer and in his service to the poor and the outcast. Yet Christ was inviting him into a thicket to receive a deeper treasure.

Thomas of Celano writes of Francis that "all the striving of this man of God, whether in public or in private, revolved around the cross of the Lord."[5] From his desire to be a knight to his calling to leave the pleasure of the world to the words of Christ crucified calling him to rebuild his Church — everything came down to the cross. "From that moment," Celano continues, "the memory of the Lord's passion was stamped on his heart with a deep brand-mark, and as conversion reached its deepest self, his soul began to melt, as his beloved spoke."[6]

Even though Francis was given this heavenly insight into the suffering of Christ, he did not boast about it. He would often hide his wounds and cover up the bleeding. He was known to only wash his fingers so others would not see his wounds, and he would wear wool socks to hide the wounds on his feet. Francis knew that sacrifice was the way of God, but he did not desire to flaunt his sacrifice to the world. It was enough for him to be with Christ in his pain. When we make offerings of sacrifice, we should also keep them private in order to foster humility as well as give a secret gift over to God.

All of this is summarized in an invitation that some of the friars speak of that sounds so simple but can make all the difference: Take the cross off the wall. Crosses are invitations. When we take a cross in our hands and stare at the One who gave his life for us, we can more clearly see the love he has for us. Crosses are nice symbols when they hang on the wall. They are good reminders of whom we should serve and what our lives should be about. But if we desire to live the cross, we have to take it off the wall and bring it close.

Following Francis means we never sanitize the cross. We cannot be afraid of the awkwardness of maybe not feeling anything right away as we hold it in our hands and stare at Christ. We have to become comfortable with being uncomfortable if we wish to begin to renew our own hearts so that we too can offer our whole selves to God. This is what Christ meant when he delivered his invitation to his disciples to carry their own crosses, because we will all have suffering and pain to endure.

What is the worst thing that has ever happened to you? What was the most pain you ever experienced (whether it be physical, emotional, or psychological)?

My answer to this, maybe like yours, comes to my mind right away. In January 2024, I received a phone call from my wife, who was at our first sonogram appointment with our third child. I got the worst news of my life. We had twins, but we had lost one baby already and the second child was displaying signs that brought heavy concern to the doctor and sonogram technician. We were told that our second child had a 50/50 chance to live and that we should come back next week to have another sonogram.

At that moment, my life changed. My vision for how I love my two sons changed, and I was hurt unlike ever before. I had lost a child. Unfortunately, miscarriage is much more common than we think. It is usually just not spoken of. The pain that a parent can experience when they have lost a child they have never met is quite unique. Knowing that I might lose two was even worse, especially since I am also a twin.

My wife and I, along with our family and friends, spent the next week in deep and desperate prayer. We were hurting, and the cross was never so real. It seemed like everything was dark and dreary. There was a weight we carried for that week. We were blessed to hear that the second child was completely healthy at our next visit, and as I write these words, we are awaiting his or her arrival.

Never before in my life had I experienced the tragic beauty of suffering. I was so hurt and in so much pain. But it made me consider, more than ever before, the pain that Jesus endured on that cross. The hurt that he felt was so real and so powerful. His suffering defeated death and sin. I never experienced the truth of the cross that the saints preach and shout about like I did during the experience of our miscarriage.

The reason I write about this is because crosses and pain are so real for each of us. The pain you are experiencing right now might feel immense and insurmountable. You might not have blood coming from your hands and feet and side, but you are being given true access to the cross of Christ. Sometimes we carry a hidden stigmata. Yet we know there is no greater love than suffering for others.

If we take the cross off the wall and fall in love with the power of the stigmata, we will unleash the power of Jesus' suffering through our own crosses. Then the light of the empty tomb will bring us joy and clarity in our need for rebuilding.

Renewal Is Most Probable When It Looks Impossible

If you take time to honestly reflect on the state of your own sinfulness, the wreckage of the political sphere, your local Church, and the global loss of faith, it might appear that we cannot come back from the faith deficit in which we reside. This project of rebuilding can seem impossible. Many events in the history of the Jewish people and Christianity can attest to something similar. We profess that the God of the universe was convicted of a capital offense and was humiliated in his suffering and death at the hands of ruthless Romans. Thousands heard him teach and heal, but only a handful of people remained at his side as he died an excruciating death.

Perhaps this is why the disciples went back to their day jobs immediately following Good Friday. They thought there was no way they were coming back from such a defeat. In fact, they feared for their lives.

In the days and months following the death of Saint Francis, remarkable things happened. There are dozens of accounts of miraculous healings that took place in the short period after his death. How were these people healed by Francis even though he was dead? They journeyed to his tomb and prayed for his intercession. These people were blind, crippled, lepers, and there are even accounts of people who were dead or at death's door who were instantly brought back to health by making contact with something that Francis had touched or by the intercession of someone who prayed for Francis's aid.

This is an important note to end on, because renewal is difficult. It is not easy to see family members, parishioners, friends, and coworkers who ignore, walk away from, or outright reject the Faith. Too often we can bring ourselves to despair and convince ourselves that the victory is not his. The miracles that came after Francis's death remind us that even in death, there is no defeat of the power of our God. If Francis can work after his death and heal others, then there is nothing — not even death — that can stop holiness from rebuilding the broken.

In fact, it is when things are most in need of repair that beginning the process of renewal is most necessary and most potent. That is the story of Francis and the story of our God who became man and rose from the dead.

Reflection Questions

- Would you describe your prayer life as intimate or formal? What are steps you can take to focus more on the way that God looks at you when you pray?
- Reread the Varanasi Letter quotation. What stands out to you the most?
- How can you bring the truth more into conversations you have with people in your ordinary life? Who are some people to whom you can commit to speak to more about the Faith and your relationship with God?
- How can you answer the invitation to suffering and humility practically in your life? What might that look like?

4
Pillars of Change

I t is difficult to believe that individuals can change, that people can actually alter the way they live. This is why we are often reluctant to believe in someone's conversion.

What do you think? Can people radically change? Have you changed much over the course of your life? If you haven't, should you? If you have, has it been for the better?

In our fight to become who we were made to be, many aspects are in the spiritual realm, while some are in the physical or intellectual sphere. When it comes to putting things into practice, we must be specific and practical. Philosophical roots of evil and theological inconsistencies have a huge impact on creating a wayward culture. As we have seen, though, our biggest issues can often be human flaws. Sin tends to have a grip on the world that feels stronger than holiness, so we must implement concrete ways to shift that trend in our hearts so we can be men and women of change in society. Christianity is not merely a practice in moral reform, but a complete renewal of the heart that depends on the work of Christ through our hands. You are the one who will change the world. He needs you.

That may sound extremely naive. One person cannot change the world, says every realist and pragmatist who has ever lived. Saint Francis would intensely disagree. In fact, there was one person, Jesus Christ, who literally changed the world and ushered in a future of possible glory for every human person that stretches into eternity. Christ called ordinary people to follow him and share the truth, peace, and love of the Father with their communities. Francis followed this call during his life, with amazing results. The recipe he followed is the same one that is called for today, and the only transformative ingredient is a commitment to ongoing personal conversion.

How did Francis change the reality of the broken world of his time and raise up men and women who were willing to give up everything to follow Jesus? How did he convince others that what he was doing, which seemed crazy to many people — living in the woods, not working, selling all his possessions, begging for food and water, etc. — was the missing link for repairing his time?

Saint Bonaventure nailed down the specific secret recipe of Francis: "Who can express the fervent charity which burned in the heart of Francis, the friend of the bridegroom? For he seemed to be absorbed, as a live coal in the furnace, in the flame of divine love."[1]

Francis was captivating because he was consumed by God's love in Christ. He was one seemingly insignificant man from a small town in Italy who simply did what God asked him to do. Look at what God can do when we accept his will for our lives. The unique power of unleashing the way of Francis is found in the fact that what Jesus asked of him is what he asks of all of us: to rebuild, to allow Christ to change our lives.

The strength to change your life, and the courage to share how deep conversion is possible and important, comes from grace. God has granted and continues to grant to his disciples the powerful capacity to relay his beautiful message of redemption to the world. Luckily, it does not depend on human intelligence or power to be effective. All that matters is that we stay true to the Gospel and lay down our lives in sincere service to the souls in our web of interactions.

Sometimes we have to preach explicitly, and sometimes we need to use ordinary human experiences to showcase the reality we know runs everything and holds everything in being. We are all invited to meet the task at hand with our sleeves rolled up and our trust in Christ. Doing so will allow Jesus to have the first word and the last say as we embark on the practical work of renewal.

If we are honest, things are falling apart in many ways. We know that the light will overcome the darkness, but wickedness surely seems powerful these days. If you are like me, you may often desire to fight against the brokenness and wickedness by attacking it head on. I can too easily become frustrated and agitated. I can be too critical instead of leaning into hope and grace. Then I end up fighting against something that is wrong, but doing so in the wrong way.

Have you ever become so annoyed at the wrong being done or said in your family, among friends, or at work that you speak up, but in a way that makes things worse? You end up making the Christian position become more alienating than appealing to those involved. This is why renewal comes about through a deeper conversion of how we think and act. This is also why we need the words and witness of Saint Francis.

Once when Francis was traveling and staying in Siena, there was also a Dominican preacher in the area. This preacher wanted to talk to Francis about the words from the prophet Ezekiel (cf. Ez 90 3:18): "If you do not warn the wicked man about his wickedness, I will hold you responsible for his soul."[2] Francis explained that he was not a learned man, but the preacher insisted on hearing his opinion. Francis finally acquiesced to the preacher's pleading. He said:

> If that passage is supposed to be understood in a universal sense, then I understand it to mean that a servant of God should be burning with life and holiness so brightly, that by the light of his example and the tongue of his conduct, he will rebuke all the wicked. In that way, I say, the brightness of his life and the fragrance of his reputation will proclaim their wickedness to all of them.[3]

You do not have to become a wizard in rhetoric and argument tactics to change the hearts of those around you. What we need is to come alive and be shining bright with the light that is Christ within us. There is a reason why people loved meeting Mother Teresa or Saint Francis. To meet them was to encounter Someone else. Their presence and words communicated that God was real and that Christ would do anything to meet them.

In order for us to be crafted into such a likeness, we will need to devote time to investigating what it means to be like Christ and to be made holy. These do not need to be lofty and abstract ideas and ideals — it all begins with small, simple choices that become the bedrock for renewal. Change begins with practical steps and concrete trust.

Habits for Holiness

Holiness is within our grasp if we rely on God and do our part. Sanctity must be the context and motive for everything that we do. This is the simple message at the heart of the wonderful book by Fr. Mark-Mary Ames, CFR, *Habits for Holiness: Small Steps for Making Big Spiritual Progress*. The practical nature and simple

challenges contained within the book's pages make it a necessary read for all contemporary Catholics desiring to grow closer
to Christ and bring others to his side amidst the troublesome
details of our age.

Habits for Holiness takes the model of Saint Francis and the
Rule of Life of the friars and shows how all Catholics, no matter
our vocation or stage in life, can use them as tools of faith in our
lives as disciples. The desire for sanctity, when put into practice,
makes all the difference. It was what moved the hearts of those
who encountered Jesus, and it is what impelled Francis to ded-
icate everything to the Lord. It was also the appeal for others to
leave everything and follow Francis in order to follow Christ.

Father Mark-Mary shines a spotlight on the core pillars of
the life and mission of the Franciscan Friars of the Renewal.
These include prayer, liturgical living, community, simplicity,
mission, and our baptismal call. Each one of these arenas flows
into the other and becomes a source for radical growth in the
spiritual life. Being grounded in one's relationship with God, living in union with others, celebrating the sacraments regularly,
and accepting Christ's call to bring his message and love to the
ends of the earth are all essential elements for the saintly life. At
the same time, the saints (like Francis) did not perform these actions so they could become saints. They simply loved Jesus, and
these actions flowed forth.

Life can feel like a constant race to get to the next thing, buy
the next thing, and get through the current day's list of responsibilities. Yet Father Mark-Mary shows that we can come to see the
profound embrace of God in every moment. *Habits for Holiness*
focuses on running the marathon of life with a dependence on
and disposition toward spiritual nourishment. The key is that
this can be accomplished in ordinary, simple ways, provided we
are intentional about growing holy habits.

A crucial aspect of the holy life is to inject Christ "strategically and prudently"[4] in one's daily practices. A constant refrain of Father Mark-Mary is the call to recognize where you are in your spiritual life and to take the next step, whatever that step may be. This is *poco a poco* or "little by little," which is the namesake for the CFRs' podcast hosted by Father Mark-Mary. (Some of the podcast's most important content will be featured in the next chapter.)

"We all frequently make plans for how to get to our goals,"[5] Father Mark-Mary explains. However, the issue most people have is strategy. Put your good intentions and holy goals into practice by working prudently and patiently toward your goal, little by little. We must have tangible goals that we can actually attain if we want to make progress in the spiritual life.

The first pillar for putting this into daily practice is something called the "3 x 5 Examen." This is a five-minute prayer that "reorients and reroutes us to reality."[6] The idea is to silently recall five things you are grateful for, five ways that you are in need of God's mercy, and five areas in your life where you desire to ask God for help. Turning inward and reflecting on our need to be thankful while asking for forgiveness and imploring God's assistance puts us in the place to be more aware and open to how God is working in our lives and how we might be impeding his love from reaching us more powerfully. This allows us to give God praise, name our sin, and acknowledge that we need his help.

The second primary pillar for repairing one's faith life in a practical way is focusing on relationship and community. For religious brothers and sisters, this takes place in the context of their religious community, but for most people this happens in the family. Father Mark-Mary explains: "What I most deeply desire is intimacy. What I most deeply desire is to be in communion with others. In other words, what I most deeply desire is family."[7] Christians are called to deep union with the Trinity, but we are also invited into the intimacy of a relationship with our family members. That is why, in God's divine wisdom, he places every human person in automatic communion with at least two people when they are born: a mother and a father. Families are where we learn how to love and how to be loved, and how to treat others. When our closest relationships flourish, they allow us to see that the needs of our neighbors should have a claim on our hearts, because everyone belongs to the same family. Family should also mean close-knit communities (of nonfamily members) that vibrantly live out the Faith. These communities should enrich our lives so we can go on mission for the Lord.

We know that Christ taught about giving to the poor constantly. Experiencing the intimacy of family should push us to reflect on how we can help meet the needs of others who are in need of practical help. It is difficult to have intimacy with God if one is struggling to obtain food and water. A life of simplicity enables the Christian to live out a practical dependence on God while also providing for the needs of others from our excess wealth. Most importantly, however, we are invited to treat the poor as living persons who deserve our respect. Living out poverty should be the result of encountering the humility of Jesus, who emptied himself for our sake.

Poverty, simplicity, and contentment are necessary qualities for a holy life. Serving the poor is not optional when it comes to being a disciple, and we all have different ways to give aid to those in need. Generosity is not optional for followers of Jesus. There is no doubt that God is giving us opportunities to pour ourselves out. Our assignment is to figure out where those opportunities are and break our lives open in love. Doing so requires a strong faith but also an intentional strategy.

If we know we are going to be spending time in a major city where we will encounter a large number of people who are homeless, we can bring granola bars and a few water bottles with us. Then when we encounter those in dire need, we can hand them food and water while introducing ourselves to them. That one-minute interaction could be the difference that allows someone to experience their dignity. It also allows us to not ignore Christ who is the one we encounter when we serve "one of these least ones" (Mt 25:40).

We can make small sacrifices so others' needs can be provided for, but we must also do everything we can to ensure that our personal encounters with the poor are opportunities for them to see the face of God through our love. When we do that, we will be surprised that the poor often have more to teach us than we have to teach them. This reminder should be humbling and centering. Christians do not serve the poor because they are charity cases. We do not help the poor so we feel better about ourselves and have more peace returning to our comfortable lifestyles. We are to give ourselves away to those most in need because that is what Jesus did, and following his example makes us who we are meant to be.

Yes, we should also do so because it changes the world; but we desire to change the world because we want to participate in God's divine plan. Discipleship is a participation in the loving providence of a Father who desperately desires for all his children to know him and be saved. Love motivates the heart and inspires the strategy.

Amidst all our daily difficulties and tasks, the details of the way of life that we are committed to by virtue of our vocation unveil God's presence. Christ's gaze is always right in front of us, in the people and circumstances of everyday life.

So we should never discount the impact that keeping to our daily responsibilities of prayer, work, and love for family can have. Whether you are a stay-at-home parent who is constantly cleaning and caring for the home, or you are an investment banker traveling on mass transit to work every day, Jesus wants to sanctify the world through the commitments we currently have. Some might be called to radically alter their own lives and career paths for the Lord, but most are called simply to be faithful in the lives we already are leading. Renewal occurs once we do ordinary tasks with a supernatural vision and perspective. We do not need to start our own YouTube channel or podcast. We do not need to become a famous Catholic speaker. All we need to do is allow Christ to work through us so he can reach the people in our lives whom he is calling by name.

Communal life is the key. God is a Divine Family of Persons, and we who are made in his image are saved through communion. We must lean on the love and presence of our community — whatever that looks like for us — if we desire to be sanctified at each step of the journey.

We are also called to poverty. Franciscan poverty may sound radical — perhaps too radical and not realistic. In Scripture, the word for Christ's call for his disciples to "deny themselves" and follow him is the Greek *arnoumai*. This is a radical word. It does not simply mean that we mentally reject wealth, but that we actually "disavow" and "denounce" money. Doing so opens us up to be Christ for all we meet.

While many people are not called to material poverty to such a degree, there is no doubt that Jesus calls every disciple to renounce his possessions (see Lk 14:33). How we do so will depend on our own discernment and circumstances. But doing so is not really optional. We are asked to consistently find ways to affirm the reality that our possessions are not ours, so we can give aid to those in need and intentionally declare our dependence on God for everything.

Whatever our state of life might be, let us begin to accept the invitation to form greater habits for sanctity so our hearts can be renewed to spread Christ's love to the edges of our society and save souls along the way.

Sacrificial Love

The only surgery I ever had in my life took place when I was twenty-three years old, to remove a post-spinal cyst from my lower back. I needed to be at the hospital at 3:50 a.m. because of the protocol for signing into surgery and filling out the necessary paperwork. My dad was the first one to volunteer to take me.

The last person I saw before I was wheeled into the operating room was my dad. He must have been able to tell that I was a little nervous about the epidural and being put under for several hours. He grabbed my face and said, "It's going to be all right, bud. I'll see you in a little bit." Before I knew it, it was all over.

As I came to my senses following the procedure, the first thing I felt were my legs pulsating. They were throbbing every few seconds. The doctors had placed compression socks on my legs to help with blood flow. Then, as the fog in my eyesight dissipated, I could hear my dad.

"Tom. Thomas. I am here. It's Dad." He had his hand on my forearm and was smiling. "You did great," he said. Then we laughed about how groggy I felt.

It didn't seem like the biggest deal at the time, but my dad woke up at 3:00 a.m. that day and was sitting in the hospital waiting for me for nearly seventeen hours by the time I was ready to be released. He told me everything went well and then said I should go back to sleep, promising he'd stay there with me. What stands out to me the most was the way he looked at me and spoke to me as I entered and came out of surgery. He was so present. He could not have been more "there for me." I always knew that my dad was in my corner, that he loved me, and that he would do anything for me. I knew I could depend on him. But going through this process made me more aware of something

I too often take for granted and overlook: My father sacrifices everything for his kids. Now that I'm a dad myself, I understand this better than I did then. When my kids are hurting or in need, I can't help but be there for them and keep my eyes on them.

I think this is what prayer is meant to communicate to us if we are open and attentive to it. When we sacrifice a little time, our heavenly Father allows us to see that he is always waiting for us and always at our side. God remains, ever present. When we see this, we realize that his presence communicates his sacrifice.

Experiencing the deep love of the Father, seeing the gaze of the Son, and being lit on fire by the strength of the Holy Spirit in prayer will carve out disciples who multiply the effects once made by Saint Francis. The most poignant cause of conversion is a witness of life that embodies the sacrificial love of a God who stops at nothing to be with his children. That unceasing love is what set Jesus apart from every other person the disciples had ever met. They did not understand it through academia or even through his teachings as much as they experienced it through his actions and tenderness. What won over the first disciples was the way Jesus looked at them. Francis knew this; he experienced it himself, and he spread it abundantly to everyone he met.

When we look at the life of a Franciscan today, we may consider it too rigorous and intense. Who can possibly make all those sacrifices and still be happy? Wouldn't normal people want to have the ordinary comforts of life? Yet that is what love does. My dad was not thinking about comfort when he woke up after only a few hours' sleep and refused to leave my side while I recovered from surgery. He was glad to make that sacrifice for me because he loves me.

The same is true for the followers of Francis today, and for each of us in our lives of faith. The witness of the Franciscan lifestyle embodies the capacity of the human person to love without counting the cost. It is like the love of a father for his child. The authentic happiness and unwavering joy the Franciscans possess is something that every human person is searching for because sacrifice taps into our true identity. We deeply desire to be fulfilled and to live heroic lives. When dealing with the brokenness of the world, this is something we must direct others to and draw out of them.

We often choose selfishness over sacrifice, the ego over God. Yet our conversations and interactions with unbelievers or cultural Catholics who do not practice the Faith should highlight the life we were made for instead of judging how a person is doing everything incorrectly. A person might be headed down the wrong path, but we can only help them to conversion when we journey with them. For this reason, Francis jumped into the garbage dumps of a sinful world to salvage the beautiful that lay hidden beneath the surface. He was interested in repairing, not condemning. This is what Jesus Christ did on Calvary, because true restoration is most concerned with repairing what is broken.

The negative way is not the answer. Rebuilding hearts and cultures begins with the perspective that nothing is ever completely lost — nothing is impossible for God (see Lk 1:37). The desire for society to return to the pride of Christendom often brews tremendous negativity. We are tempted to believe it would be so much better and so much easier if everyone just agreed with the positions we held. Following Jesus, however, is not merely an admittance and assent to a philosophical outlook on life. Discipleship is about the heart.

We long for the world to be good and just, but oftentimes God wants to use us in the process. We should turn from sin and do good, but we should never turn our back on the sinner. We don't give up because Jesus asks us not to give up. We stay committed, focused, and optimistic because he will, undoubtedly, bring about his kingdom. Optimism does not mean naivete.

Optimism means we are a people of hope and joy because we know Jesus will restore all — everything is his.

We help forward Jesus' project when we act from an intentional spirit of sacrifice every single day. Who in my life most needs God? Who has gone astray? Will I see them today? How have I treated them lately? How would they describe how I carry myself and treat them?

Sacrifice means we have a game plan for how we can best portray the love of Christ to those who are in most need of his grace and mercy. Sacrifice means we place our egos to the side and throw ourselves into the details of another person's life so they know we care about them. Those on the team of restoration must be apostles who desire to be sent to those in need simply because we want them to know they are known and loved by God. This might be the largest sacrifice we are called to offer in our life.

Christians can romanticize sacrifice as much as they can turn Saint Francis into an irrelevant figure who spoke to some animals and said some prayers. The sacrifice of his life was not that simple; it was so much more. His consistent decision to care for the souls in front of him came from a deep awareness of the love behind the sacrifice of Christ on the cross. That was the motivation for his daily sacrifices and penance. Jesus' suffering is the motivation for any great saint. The deep knowledge the saints had of Jesus' depth of love made it easy for them to love as he did — to break themselves open as he did.

We can break ourselves open by interacting lovingly with those in our lives who disagree with the Faith. We might be guilty of occasionally being so caught up in winning over their minds that we forget they are people for whom we are called to love and sacrifice, not cases to be won. Talking to others about the Faith is not "work." We are invited to make our faith a natural part of who we are, not merely a matter for conversation and argument. Sharing our faith has to be about more than social work and meeting people's material needs. The goal is to help others become holier, and holiness comes about when people are united to God, not won over in an argument.

So, a self-reflection process is necessary. Think about the people in your life who most need Jesus Christ. It could be family members, a spouse, or coworkers. You might be one of the only people from whom they hear the Christian message. Do they think your conversations with them are more about winning an argument than about loving them? Do they think you are judgmental? In what ways might you need to work on simply caring for them and being in a friendship with them, rather than treating them like cases to be solved? Can you sacrifice more for them?

The renewal process is not about making people who we want them to be; it is about helping them become who God made them to be, even as we allow God and our community to turn us into the people we were created to be. That is why all the miracles in the Gospels are amazing: yes, Jesus performs something unexplainable, but he also calls people by name and knows their situations better than they themselves do.

When faced with issues in our society and in the Church, we must always err on the side of sacrificial love, which makes us more like Jesus. This does not mean we bow before the powers of evil that have taken over our world in many ways. It simply means that we live and move and have our being from the standpoint of trust in a Father who has already saved the world. Our participation in the salvation of souls must rest on this foundation if we want it to be effective.

Service to the Other

Sacrifice is a mentality that leads to practical service.

Every one of us has a specific task that God is counting on us to accomplish, because each human person is unrepeatable, irreplaceable, and unique in the eyes of the Father. This should not inflate our pride, but should humble us and drive us to ensure that every single person experiences this reality.

The great saints all possessed an uncanny ability to be strong and sacrifice for others. We often think their uniqueness lay in their unusual strength. In reality, their greatness came from their perspective, not their fortitude. Since they were people of deep prayer, they knew God was real and that he loved them into existence. If this was true for them personally, then it is also true for every other person on the planet. Every individual they met was an immortal soul that was worth the very life of God. This is what the cross tells us. This vision gave them the awareness that service is not something we have to do but a beautiful chance to ratify and affirm the worth of every human being.

Do we give ourselves away in humble and radical service as much as we can? Do we serve with joy, or do we complain about having to do the tasks no one else is willing to do? These are not accusations, but a necessary gut check to reveal how we can be more heartfelt about renewal. Service is ultimately an act of charity that is concerned with the good of the other. The good of the world is in the balance, and we have a role to play that no one else can fill. Simple and humble service will change the world.

This is what we celebrate with the Incarnation at Christmas and the suffering of Jesus on Good Friday. Jesus breaks himself open and pours himself out by becoming an infant and by allowing his life to be taken. He does so to reveal just what God's nature is. The Trinity is an endless and perfect relationship of self-giving love; it is an infinite process of emptying out. This is why God appears, by the standards of the world, to be small and insignificant. He came to us two thousand years ago born of peasants from Nazareth, and he died as a criminal convicted of a capital offense. He dwells in bread and wine that, by all appearances, is nothing unique. God continually allows himself to be viewed as small and insignificant. He continues to allow himself to be overlooked because love cannot be forced.

Once the truth of his presence and the grandeur of his quiet humility is recognized, however, it changes everything. Love always appears weak by human standards because it depends on acceptance, not force or power. So God comes to us one at a time, and he searches for us to follow him. He calls us by name and invites us to become humble and seemingly insignificant like him, because it is in our nature to become grafted to his nature. So salvation continues one person at a time, because God's language is humble service, and this is how he redeems us.

Both convey the truth that humble service to God and others is what is most needed. Too often we concern ourselves with things we cannot change, and this prevents us from impacting the world in ways we actually can. Large movements of renewal that work always come from the ground up, so they remain humble. If everyone did their part to be like God in humility, the entire world would be changed.

We can also be too worried about looking different to a world that values fitting in and being accepted more than anything else. Francis wanted to be a fool for Christ. This was a badge of honor that he wore because he knew the world rejected Jesus, so it would also reject anyone who lived from a place of close union with the Lord. Being lowly was a good thing; it was a reward for Francis.

All is God's. This is what God continues to communicate to us sojourners. Despite the anxieties of life, the challenges of raising a family today, and the need for deep conversion in our Church, God will reign victorious. The answer is not our greatness, but his glory shining through our everyday actions and words. This is what will make us both holy and credible.

Being emphatically fascinated with following Jesus and his

teachings will make us like Francis, who was completely conformed to Christ. It sounds too simple to actually make a difference, but it is the truth of the rebuilding process. Do we appear like Christ to this world? Praying novenas and being people of deep spirituality is fine and good, but are we more like the Pharisees than we might like to admit? Is it possible that our vision of the world and our appearance before the world need to be repaired? Are we people of deep service and sacrifice, or of self-righteousness and ego?

Mother Teresa, when asked how a person can change the world, said, "Go home and love your family." No other person on the planet has access to the exact group of relationships that you do. Your family might be shared with your siblings and your parents, but your family does not know all your friends or coworkers. Your friends don't have intimate relationships with your family while your coworkers likely don't know either group. There is a beautiful exchange and ripple effect when each individual takes ownership of impacting the lives around him or her. If every person did this, the ripples would spread worldwide.

Service begins with loving the very next person as much as we can by affirming his dignity, as Francis would do, and by giving witness to God's glory in our own lives. There will come a time when we will need to speak with others about the specifics of conversion, but we must always remember not to place the cart before the horse, treating people like they are a match we want to win. Mother Teresa also knew this, and she was not being facetious when she called on us to go love our families. She revealed two critical components of restoration in the simplicity of her answer.

First, we can become so distraught about the big picture of the world that we forget to care for those around us. Francis never allowed this. He knew that when we focus too much on grand issues in politics or in the Church, we neglect the aspects of life that are actually in our control. One of the most practical, inspirational, and transformative tips that can be drawn out from the spirit of Saint Francis is to constantly ask ourselves what our focus is.

Are we spending the majority of our time stressing about things we can never actually change? Do national headlines and the gossip of the Church rule our lives, or do the needs of our spouses, families, and parishes claim our hearts? Francis lived emphatically for the present moment, and that is how he changed the world. We do not have to accept brokenness as the final answer for our world. We must face the darkness of our age, but we also must shine the light in the darkness.

The second truth Mother Teresa showed with her words was that the family is the biggest contributor to infusing faith and virtuous habits into society. Her dear friend, Pope St. John Paul II, once said in a homily in his travels to Singapore, "As the family goes, so goes the nation and so goes the whole world in which we live." Creating a strong fabric of disciples in the home is the best, and possibly only, way to send servants of God into the culture who will instill Christian virtues wherever they go. Therefore, we must serve and be attentive to the needs of our family. For those of us who are parents, we must do this also so our children can become men and women who perform healing works for the next generation.

Finally, we must ask the million-dollar question: How does one fuel service? While Christ will supply us with the capacity to live as his disciples, our own personal choice will play a huge role in how this is lived out practically. The best thing we can do is continue to try to maintain the joyful disposition that Christ is always victorious. When we fail to serve or act from that place, we must pick ourselves up and try again, because restoring the world is also the way that we will become more deeply converted ourselves.

Let Mercy Reign

No one is defined by their worst sin or mistake.

When we miss the mark in our call to be like Christ, we must count on God's loving and infinite forgiveness, just as Saint Francis did. The more we remember and live from the reality of God's Presence, the more we can change the world. So we must be strong in our expectations, and we must emulate characteristics of sanctity embodied so well in Saint Francis.

But what happens when we fall short? What happens when others who we love or even others that we hardly know fall short? What happens when our Church and our country become dangerously flawed? We have to let mercy rule our lives. Sin separates us from God, and many of us respond poorly when we sin ourselves or when we are faced with sin in those around us. The soil that allows sin to grow is a lack of trust in God's goodness. Therefore, the separation that we experience from God in our sin is ultimately tied up with the human refusal to trust God (especially when sin is ruling the circumstances surrounding us).

Sometimes we don't really believe that God is for us or that we can truly count on him. So we become selfish and prideful and angry at how the world has fallen. We may even become self-centered because we think the world needs to become more like us. Maybe pride drives our every thought and action because we believe only we have the recipe that will fix things in our families or in our parish. All of this leads us to become bitter and angry toward those we encounter each day.

All these examples move us away from mercy. St. Faustina Kowalska would often note that one of the biggest hurts that Christ experiences is the rejection of his mercy by those who need it the most. Our first assumption should be that we are the ones who need his mercy the most — not because we are necessarily the worst sinners, but because his mercy is an endless well from which he desires us to draw life. Mercy will convert and rebuild the Church and the world. That will only happen when we learn to trust more radically.

We need Jesus. Francis knew this, and it is why he gravitated toward poverty and humility. It was why he prayed unceasingly. He knew that life is about being dependent on God's mercy. When we figure that out, we become more open to how God desires to move our heart and move in our lives.

Selfishness, pride, and anger rule the attitudes of the faithful who, deep down, don't really trust that God is a good Father who will never, ever fail us. Francis would not allow the needs of the world to distract him from trusting. In fact, he saw humanity's inability to heal itself as stronger proof that we need to rely on Jesus' mercy. That is why the poor and the outcast were his main focus. They needed God in some of the most simple and practical ways so they could be rebuilt in his image and likeness.

Who is the outcast in your life? Every week reflect on how you could have been more present and more like Francis to those whom you encounter every day. Consider how you can be practically loving and merciful to those who are most often ignored. This might include people who are struggling with profound sin.

Jesus is divine, and while on earth he immersed himself in sinful surroundings. He never became what was around him, but he always desired to invade the darkness at the same time. Living this truth in imitation of Jesus transforms us into kingdom-bearers, just as it did for Saint Francis. Just as salt brings out the flavor of food, Christians are called to bring out the best in the world and in their circumstances. This is what mercy does. It places a spotlight on human dignity, and it calls forth the best in others.

Jesus also says that we must become like children if we wish to inherit the kingdom of God (see Mt 18:3). We must rely on the goodness of God and trust radically in his providence. We must do our part, and then we must rest in the reality that God will do the rest. We are not the ones who are responsible for saving the world.

That is where mercy comes in. Mercy takes care of the rest, but it does not simply wipe clean the sins or brokenness that is willfully chosen. This is critical: Mercy is not automatic forgiveness that neglects the rules of justice. Mercy echoes the chorus that your worst sin does not define you. Jesus wants in on your worst quality or most tragic sin. Christ desires to run toward you when you are at your weakest and ugliest. Mercy does not give up on the wildest sinner or the horrendous qualities of our country and Church because mercy, like water, always (always) finds the lowest point.

Jesus' encounter with the woman at the well showcases this point beautifully. She has had so many husbands, she is ashamed of herself, and she is trying to escape her shame. Enter Jesus, who reveals to her that the view she has of her self-worth and identity could not be further from the truth. The way he looks at her and the words he conveys are strong, but warm. They are challenging, but also affirming.

Christ came to Samaria just to meet a nameless woman who lived a life full of serious mistakes. Jesus also comes to us each day and offers us the same mercy. Once we recognize just how much we need it, that mercy will propel us to pave avenues of mercy within all our own relationships as well. Who is your woman at the well?

God is always there; that is what the cross teaches us. For this reason, Jesus exclaimed: "For where two or three are gathered together in my name, there am I in the midst of them" (Mt 18:20). No one has ever been completely alone because God gives us each other to help us see that he is with us always. That is why our sacrifice and service is so pivotal. That is why we are called to do our part, like Francis, in restoring the world to the sanctity God desires. The way of Francis is not a call for charity in a strictly worldly sense. It is a rallying cry for the faithful to act as the face of mercy to a hurting world.

Mercy is the abiding presence of God. Francis personified that mystery, and he lived out the grandeur encapsulated in the fact that Jesus is consistently "in our midst." Living like that takes prayer, vigilance, and practice, but its effects run wild when even just a few people accept the invitation with vigor. The impact of Saint Francis is living proof of just how possible those effects and changes are in our world.

Reflect

- What are some changes in your own life, the lives of others you know, or the culture that you find to be insurmountable? How can you hand those over to God like Francis did?
- What are some bad habits you need to break that are getting in the way of your personal holiness and conversion? What are some habits that you desire to implement based on the witness of St. Francis of Assisi?
- Are you leaning more toward selfishness than sacrifice in some areas of your life? What can you do to become more Christ-like in this area?
- Do you struggle more with service or with showing mercy? Whichever one is more difficult for you, focus on that for this upcoming week and see the difference it makes.

5
Franciscan Friars of the Renewal

As Saint Francis neared the end of his life, he would often declare to the brothers the same line, over and over again: "Let us begin again to serve the Lord because up to now we have done nothing." With all that he had done and started, he always knew that there was more to do, because he saw his life's task as an invitation to announce God's presence and power.

This was not a dependence on his own ministry or power, but a true realization that the work of the disciple is a continuous endeavor. Ministry was not a job for Francis, not something he could retire from; ministry was discipleship. Being present to the lost, the least, and the outcast is the mission of every disciple. Francis deeply understood the ramifications of even one person not fulfilling his calling. For this reason, Francis consistently spoke about how idleness is the enemy of the soul. Failing to act for the love of God and others has eternal ramifications.

Francis's life was consumed by action. He was compelled

to act once he received the message from Jesus on the crucifix. He spent hours in intimate prayer each day. He began dragging boulders to mend the structure of San Damiano. He was urged forth to serve the lepers and the poor in his community. Francis was convinced that to follow Jesus meant that every movement and footstep was for the humble savior of the world.

Conversion and renewal are all about beginning again, each and every day.

Francis's words in his final days were also the result of the fact that he knew he had further to go on the path of repentance, as we all do. Amazingly enough, even the great saint of Assisi yearned to be closer to God before his death. He wanted every sinful inclination and selfish tendency to be completely driven out of him. It was not good enough for him to simply be "fine" or "good enough" in his actions. He wanted to be perfect as Christ called him — and calls each one of us — to be (Mt 5:48).

Toward the end of his life, Fr. Benedict Groeschel would often say: "I just wish … there has to be more time." Those who knew him well would say that he was a man who would, too often, schedule thirty hours of ministry and work into a twenty-four-hour day. He loved his work because he loved being with people and serving God. Every single person he met was an unrepeatable being crafted by the Father for glory, and Father Benedict always desired to have that person shine and help them to see all that they were made for.

Father Benedict did not simply want more time to do what he desired. He wanted more time so he could serve Christ and bring others to him. That was the sole fascination of his life. He knew that this was Jesus' great call to action. The Franciscan Friars of the Renewal (CFRs) are continuing this same call today. As Francis urged, they are "beginning again" every day because they yearn to be like Francis and bring others to know and love Jesus Christ.

Let's take a look at just how they do that. If modern men and women desire to put the holy example of Saint Francis into action today, we should lean on some of Francis's students who have mastered the art of repairing their individual hearts and the hearts of others. For this reason, in this chapter we will examine the work of the CFRs. There are other Franciscan orders doing great work today, but the CFRs offer a particularly poignant example of Francis's way of life. Their ministry is fed by Francis's living of the Gospel and following closely in the footsteps of Christ. The CFRs have taken up the witness of Saint Francis while implementing his wisdom and love in a manner that is, quite frankly, unmatched. Looking to their example will aid our mission of rebuilding the brokenness in our Church and in the world.

Fr. Benedict Groeschel

The CFRs were founded as a religious order in 1987. Father Benedict and several other brothers were the core group behind the movement. They would be Capuchin friars living in the spirit of Saint Francis in the world by focusing on reforming the Church and caring for the poor.

The first community of friars lived in the South Bronx, in an area known as Fort Apache because of the crime and violence that was rampant there. The goal of the brothers was to live like Francis, to be deeply dedicated to a life of prayer and service to the poor. That meant they were going to serve, love, and care for those in Fort Apache.[1]

Choosing their first home to be in such a dark and difficult place highlights what the CFRs are all about: shining a light in the darkness. They desire to begin each day humbly walking with Christ and those who need him most. They commit to communal prayer with the brothers and priests they live with. Then they spend their day interacting with the poor who live in their community while also ministering to the lowly in their shelters. They purposefully live among the poor because they choose to be poor with the ones they serve.

Father Benedict was born in New Jersey in 1933. As a young boy, he felt a deep call to the priesthood. He later served at a home for children with emotional needs in Dobbs Ferry, NY. He was also the cofounder of Trinity Retreat House for struggling priests and an organization called Courage, which serves those struggling with same-sex attraction while trying to live out Church teaching. His founding of the friars was simply the peak of his dedication to serving the Church and those in need.

The most helpful insights into Father Benedict will come from viewing his actual words. Here, we will highlight his words in an interview with Ignatius Press in 2004. The interview took place only months after he was struck by a car, resulting in serious injuries.

Father Benedict articulated the major spiritual source for the confusion and trouble of our time: "Unfortunately, in recent years and for peculiar reasons, there has been a loss of profound awareness of the divinity of Christ and of its real meaning. When you lose this, you also lose His humanity. His humanity doesn't make a lot of sense unless He is divine." Saint Francis knew this deeply, and it motivated everything he did. The CFRs are seen as dynamic in their Christian faith because they perform every action from this bold claim and validate its truth through their words and actions. Viewing their habits from afar and seeing their schedule of prayer and service to the poor reveals that they hold Christ to be King and Lord. Jesus is the God of their lives. They worship him and him alone. This impels them to live radically for others but also to be intense in their commitment to a relationship with Jesus. Everything begins with their commitment to prayer. In their Constitutions, their section on daily prayer notes, "Each day, the friars are to devote two one-hour periods to personal prayer." This does not include the daily celebration of the Eucharist. Contact with Jesus is non-negotiable. Their Constitution later states:

> As sons of Saint Francis in need of daily conversion, the friars are called as individuals and as a community to do penance. They thus are to live in a way that authenticates their Franciscan vocation. Their life of penance is meant to foster a perfect readiness to give themselves generously in mind, heart, and body. This generous gift of self is to enable the friars to take initiative in embracing the demands of their way of life without complaining and in a spirit that gives witness to the joy of the Lord.

Between their prayer and devotion and commitment to sacrificial love, the friars' bind themselves to the One who renews it all. "When we approach Christ," Father Benedict said, "He is the great bridge between the human race and eternity and God. A suspension bridge has two great towers; one is as essential to the bridge as the other, and the tension between them is what keeps the roadway solid and passable." He continued, "Christian dogma of the divinity of Christ, worked out in the early ecumenical councils, is like a great suspension bridge. Damage one tower and you ruin the whole bridge."

Everything the friars do, in the spirit of Saint Francis, makes this reality clear and real. Christ is the bridge between their individual hearts and God, and he is the reason why the CFRs are transforming other lives in practical ways. For this reason, the entire starting point for everything the friars do is ongoing, personal conversion, as it should be for us.

When Jesus is the center of your life, in word and in deed, then your discipleship is lit on fire. Only then can you be another Christ, as Saint Francis was. Only then can your witness be a testimony to true discipleship.

"The best way to communicate the truth of faith to people," Father Groeschel notes, "is by devotion because they are personally and emotionally, as well as intellectually, involved in what they believe." Our dedication to prayer and worship, reliance on Sacred Scripture, and fascination with Christ will resonate with the human hearts around us when we make devotion more organically a part of our own existence. The proof is in the impact of the friars. Their life could be summed up in one word: devotion. Their prayer is not forced or fabricated. It is scheduled and a part of the habit of their life. Then it becomes something that is freeing and that fuels holiness. We see from their example that devotion springs from being who we were made to be as God's creatures who consistently turn to him as Father.

Father Benedict continues, "I wish there were some way that I could convince everybody in the world that they should turn to Jesus Christ. They need Him, they look for Him, and they have a profound attraction to Him, when they have any opportunity to know Him as He is." The inclination to seek Jesus out, and the instinctual desire to be loved by him, are built into human nature, but they can also be denied and ignored. Human sin, laziness, and indifference can prevent conversion. Following Jesus is difficult. It requires that we give Jesus everything that we are. This is partially about our human effort but more so about giving Christ our hearts.

Since sacrifice and suffering play such a large role in the lives of believers and unbelievers, Father Benedict spoke about it frequently. He said, "You have to be careful with suffering. One has to be careful not to enjoy it, or focus on it, or expand it too much. Then suffering becomes the goal. The goal is not suffering; the goal is loving patience, offered to God as best one can. And the humility to admit that we don't do this very well."

Commenting on the suffering of old age and the struggles

following his accident, Father Benedict said, "One of the things I learned from my illness is that over and over again we have to tell God that we really trust Him. Trusting in God is not one action; it's an ongoing way of life." Many sufferings are given to the followers of Jesus. Usually, they are not chosen. We are called to carry these crosses as Francis did: to lift them high and unite them to Jesus' cross. At the same time, we should never make the suffering an end in itself. That "loving patience" that Father Groeschel mentions is what Francis lived by. This quality is what makes a follower of the way of Saint Francis someone who clings to the crosses of their lives out of love for Christ. That is why Francis was given the stigmata. Francis was so entrenched in the heart of Christ that he physically experienced some of the savior's pain. He did not choose this suffering; it was gifted to him. In the same way, we do not choose the crosses we are given. But when we carry them with and for Jesus, we impact others' hearts like Jesus did.

To battle the brokenness in our world, we must focus on Christ, on true devotion, and on the need for suffering as a way to enter into the experience of Jesus. Saint Francis knew this and lived it radically. Following in his footsteps, Father Benedict and the CFRs show us how powerful this way of life can be in the Church and the world today.

The impact that Father Benedict had on the Church and the influence he continues to have through the charism of the CFRs is amazing, but not surprising. Today they have fifteen friaries in North America, Central America, and Europe. There are roughly 140 friars and thirty-five Franciscan Sisters of the Renewal. The sisters were founded in 1988 with a similar charism to the friars. Ultimately, it is not their numbers that are earth-shattering, but their witness. They are living close to the way of Francis and thus walking in the footprints of Jesus. The interactions these men and women have with their communities is what is slowly changing souls. When the faith of Saint Francis is channeled well, it has outstanding consequences, because it is ultimately a laser focus on becoming like Christ in all things.

A Rule of Life

What rules your life? What consumes your thoughts, words, and actions?

Every religious order has a rule of life. This is a document that encapsulates the mission of the order while outlining how its members are to live out the details of their lives. We referenced the Constitutions or Rule of Life earlier, but diving more into the details of these words will benefit our mission here. St. Benedict of Nursia is the father of Western monasticism who wrote one of the first rules of life. He actually wrote it for lay men and women, not for religious brothers or sisters. The goal of the rule was to inject prayer and faith into everything one does by living for God at each moment.

The Rule of Life for the CFRs gives beautiful insights into who these men and women are and how they are called to renew the world in the spirit of Saint Francis. Each member ought to live out a deep desire for personal and communal renewal while reforming the life of the Church. To accomplish the restoration of faith in the world is to constantly return to the foundations of the Christian life (the Bible, prayer, service to the poor, the Eucharist, the Rosary, etc.) by taking inspiration from the life of Francis.

What does living out this Rule of Life do to someone? In the CFR Rule of Life, their section on Apostolic Mission explains, "The primary mission of the Institute is a wholehearted embracing of Jesus Christ, following the example of Our Holy Father, Saint Francis. By means of God's grace, the friars respond to his call for continuing conversion. They bear witness to God's love and reign in their lives essentially through the witness of their words and deeds." Their mission is to belong completely and un-reservedly to God. That is why the word *renewal* is in their name.

One of Francis's earliest followers, Bernard, said the following in some of his final words: "I am not able to speak to you at length. But remember that where I am, you will soon be also; and I tell you that for nothing in this world, or for a thousand worlds like this, would I wish to have lived otherwise than I have done, nor have served any other master than our Lord Jesus Christ."[2]

A Franciscan friar's life is meant to convey that our existence is a pilgrimage of committed faith, trusting hope, and effective love. They live out these three characteristics of Christianity through an attentiveness to the reality and power of the Holy Spirit. Christ's breath enlivens the mission of the CFRs and spurs them on to do their best in facilitating authentic encounters with the love of God amidst the brokenness of the world. Faith, hope, and love are the ink of the rule.

Work and poverty confine them to tasks and restrictions that they do not necessarily get to choose. There are certain duties in the friary or community that must be performed. Friars own nothing other than some absolute necessities. While they do not have careers like lay men and women, they do have schedules that are filled with responsibilities. Others depend on them to accomplish their responsibilities, but they receive no salaries.

The spirit of Francis is behind this rule because, possessing nothing, these men and women become entirely focused on the present moment. Their poverty makes them Christ-like. They are freed from the race for possessions because they are poor. All that they do is wrapped up in seeing how Christ is inviting them to rebuild their own lives and the lives around them through a surrender to ordinary and lowly tasks. Like Francis, the friars of today are immersed in the communities in which they live, recognizing that these are the people they are called to serve and evangelize.

The CFRs also commit themselves to personal and communal renewal while being continually reminded that their community life is *the* pathway forward for the deepening of their own personal conversion. They live as a family. The Lord called individual disciples by name, but they formed a group that would follow him together. They would depend on one another along the journey, and so do the friars. No one can meet the struggles of life alone. So the daily encounters of the brothers are a mixture of normal and extraordinary. They cook and clean for one another, but they also rejoice and cry with one another.

Franciscan living is grounded in the original rule of Saint Francis and in the powerful testament of the life of Francis. Observing the gospel truths means that one simply learns and listens to the words and actions of Jesus Christ found in the Bible and in the lives of his saints throughout the ages. Francis habitually trained his heart to do this. Over time, that made following Christ an instinct for him. For this reason, the CFRs have a life of habits that serve as guardrails, but they are not chores. Discipleship is not a chore or an empty list of actions for the friars, but a way of life. Discipleship is living with Jesus; it is residing with the family of Nazareth through their own family of friars.

Living in community with others is the pivotal characteristic of the Franciscan way of life. A special family bond is formed among the brothers and sisters because what unites them is their faith and common goal. They are bound together by Jesus. The houses they live in are meant to have a peaceful, prayerful, and joyful spirit. Living as a family means that the demands of others are never viewed as a burden (even when things are not perfect). Therefore, the CFRs are called to be radically open to interruptions that reveal where God is at work in their day. Each member is called to love the other, especially those in the community who are elderly, injured, or in need.

Stating a focus on faith as a relationship and the need to live in a family of faith is not something new, nor is it necessarily radical. They are ordinary things, and these ordinary things are what set the friars apart. Francis would often refer to himself as "a little one." He was a little one because he was simply following the little things.

Poverty, Chastity, Obedience

The CFRs specifically consecrate themselves to an attempt to portray the glory of heaven here on earth. They are meant to live their whole life participating in the holiness of the Trinity. They accomplish this by making the vows of poverty, chastity, and obedience. Each one of these vows, though lived through religious life, can teach lay men and women how to live the way of Francis in today's world. Every Christian is called to some level of poverty, chastity, and obedience.

Franciscan poverty is deeply physical. Each of the CFRs possesses only two religious habits for dress. They all wear simple beards and sandals. Before their entrance into the community, they are to give up all money and property that they own. Their friaries have no luxuries, they own nothing, and they depend on the generosity of donors just like Francis did. This breeds a reliance on Divine Providence that is dramatic but also simple.

The CFRs' poverty is founded upon Saint Francis's move to become more like Christ, who "humbled himself" for our sake (see Phil 2:8). Francis lived as a pilgrim and stranger in this world, so his followers do the same. Poverty is absolutely central to the life of the friars, and they are called to perform "poverty checks" to examine their lives and see if they are living in line with how Francis lived. To be poor means that they are dependent on God for all things and in all things.

Chastity gives the friars the unique capacity of having an undivided heart in their ministry. Every single person they encounter becomes the most important soul in front of them. By living the evangelical counsel of chastity, they become more like Christ (and Francis, in imitation of Christ), only concerned with the person in front of them. Intentional faith fosters being more intentional in our relationships with others. Due to the nature of chastity, it must be continuously safeguarded and nourished by emptying oneself out in prayer and sacrificial service. It requires that the friars live a life of continual conversion and a life of self-emptying love. This does not mean that the friars have to try harder than the average Catholic; they are simply invited daily to keep the spotlight on Jesus Christ. It is that simplicity that brings about the beauty of their lifestyle.

The friars' commitment to obedience is a daily reminder to them and a witness to the rest of us that the entire journey of the Christian life is to do the will of God. This is where human flourishing, holiness, and true joy reside. Jesus was obedient unto death, so the friars submit their wills to their superiors, who act as the agents of Christ's will for their lives. The renunciation of their own wills is meant to open them up to give praise to the greater glory of God.

Saint Francis once explained obedience by using the example of a dead body that cannot show any form of resistance:

> It will not murmur at the place thou gave it, nor cry out if thou leave it there. If thou shall place it on a throne, it will not look upwards but always downwards. If thou cloth it in purple, it will but look the paler. This is it with a truly obedient man. If he'd be removed, he considers not where for; he cares not where he's placed, nor asks to be transferred to another office. If he be exalted, he preserves his accustomed humility; and accounts himself the more unworthy the greater honor he receives.[3]

The Rule of Life of the CFRs showcases how the friars have become beacons of hope. There is a deep beauty and attractiveness to becoming humble like Jesus. Franciscans are convinced that if we want to rebuild the brokenness of the earth, then the best step forward is for disciples to look and act like Christ first; that is the whole meaning of conversion. That is the life of a Franciscan Friar of the Renewal.

The CFRs' Rule of Life continues with descriptions of how they are to repair the communities in which they live and work. Saint Francis knew that any effort to save souls is really God's work through our hands. Nothing holy can be done without God's anointing. This means any renewal will be the result of being grounded in a life of authentic prayer, both private and communal. The CFRs are asked to spend two hours each day in the Presence of the Blessed Sacrament. One time period is individual, and one is communal. The Sacrifice of the Mass is to be attended every day because it is the ultimate expression of the Faith and of one's unity with Christ. The utmost reverence and devotion is to be shown when praying at Mass.

According to their rule, prayer should be the very heart of the life of a friar. In their private prayer, the friars are asked to focus on the needs of all, especially the pope, bishops, and all religious. They are also asked to spend much time praying for the dead. Each month, the friars must make at least one day of solitude. This is when they leave the friary and have a day of silent prayer, on their own. These days are meant to be the springboard for their commitment to prayer during the month and a way to recharge their love for Christ. All their prayer is meant to serve at the altar of intimacy with Christ.

Penance

A life of penance is the final characteristic that I'd like to showcase for the CFRs. They do not beat themselves up, but they do live by the true claim that we are called to be content with the minimum necessary, not the maximum allowed. There are also countless practical demands on the human person that are opportunities for penance. The friars can make an offering of themselves when the traffic or noise of their neighborhood is relentless, when they do not get as much sleep as they would like, or with the many other demands that religious life inflicts on them. Their overall attitude is to cheerfully accept the sacrifices of time and energy that are imposed on them because of their mission to save souls. Penance is meant to increase the generosity of their mind and soul.

Accepting sacrifice expands the human heart. The friars attempt to live this out through their large commitments of prayer, communal life, and penance. This is their fuel.

Deep Humility and the Francis Appeal

Those who first followed in the footsteps of Saint Francis quickly became known as the Friars Minor. The word *minor* was chosen to emphasize the characteristic of Christ that Francis was most captivated by: humility. His inclination toward humility was a wellspring for everything he did. From living with and caring for lepers, giving aid to the poor, and offering back his life as a continual sacrifice to the Father, Francis was obsessed with being humble. True Christian humility arises from the recognition that the more I empty myself, the more I will become like God.

Saint Francis desired to be known as "a new type of fool for the Lord." G. K. Chesterton wrote in his biography of Saint Francis that it was the saint of Assisi's view of the world that made him appear as a fool. Chesterton recalled that "we used to be told in the nursery that if a man were to bore a hole through the center of the earth and climb continually down and down, there would come a moment at the center when he would seem to be climbing up and up."[4] Francis was able to see the world upside down, but as it truly was. Viewing everything from this point of view allowed him to see that the world was hanging on by a string — a string of complete and utter dependence on the mercy of God. Humility gives us access to this divine vision of Francis and his followers. The manner in which Francis approached life came from having the correct view of the world. He saw things as God does. and he saw humanity's dependence on God for absolutely everything. As a result of that clear vision, he traveled toward deeper conversion each day. Francis saw that being humble and lowly was the right way to live, because it was the only way that was aligned with the truth of who he was: a son of the Father. Nothing was more evident than his need to be in right relationship with God. He was truly "minor," and this truth makes the way of Francis credible and attractive in today's world, just as it was in his age.

Minority and credibility are two characteristics that define the Franciscan way. Being "minor" means that I have a humble awareness that I am not better than anyone else. Francis would say this was true even when he was calling a person to repent and convert. Even though he was asking people to return to God, that did not mean he was better than they. Francis knew he was just as broken as any sinner and that he had not crossed the finish line yet. He would note that the only reason he was able to speak about conversion was because of the mercy of God, not because he was a person of any type of greatness.

Francis would often remind the friars:

No one should flatter himself with big applause for doing something a sinner can do. A sinner can fast, he can pray, he can weep, he can mortify his flesh. But this he cannot do: remain faithful to his Lord. So this is the only reason for boasting: If we return to God the glory that is his; if we serve him faithfully and credit him for what he has given us.[5]

Thomas of Celano (the original biographer of Francis) once said, "I consider blessed Francis the holiest mirror of the holiness of the Lord, the image of his perfection. I think everything about him, both his words and deeds, is fragrant with the presence of God."[6] Humility gives God and the friars the permission to act in and through them.

Being at the feet of others was the most prized place for Francis because that is the position that Jesus took. Francis would also say that if a brother was removed from the office of washing people's feet and another brother was removed from the office of superior, that the brother who lost the foot-washing position should be more upset than the superior. The place of humility, the location of being last and servant of all, should always be sought after because that is where Christ resides most potently. That is where we can smell his fragrance and have it rub off on us. That is why Franciscans are to be "minor."

In fact, Francis once told a bishop that he did not wish for his followers to ever gain worldly offices:

> My lord, my brothers are called lesser precisely so they will not presume to become greater. They've been called this to teach them to stay down to earth, and to follow the Prince of Christ's humility, which in the end will exalt them above others in the sight of the saints. If you want them to bear fruit in the Church of God, keep them in the status in which they were called and hold them to it. Bring them back down to ground level even against their will.[7]

This type of life is not only true to Jesus, but it is immensely attractive because of its proximity to the nature of God. For this reason, Pope Pius XI once said that Francis appeared "to his contemporaries and to future generations almost as if he were the Risen Christ."[8] Such humility made him like Christ and made Francis's way attractive to all he met. It is absolutely convincing when you encounter a person living so radically like the friars because they are living with and like Christ. They lay down their lives before each person with whom they come into contact. This is not an act, but a mode of living that has Jesus at its root. Francis and his followers were never shaken by the weakness they found in others because they were so aware of the weakness in themselves. This is why Francis had so much appeal to his contemporaries, and it is what the CFRs give witness to today.

Despite all its challenges, our society still does not approve of those who place themselves before others. No one actually enjoys being around an egomaniac. No one in his right mind wants to idolize snobbery and conceit. We do not like those who alienate others. Even when our discipleship calls people to radically change their ways, this call must be grounded in the truth that all of us need to change our lives. This is both true and attractive.

Begin and End in the Desert

In Lent of 2022, the CFRs released a book for men called *Born of Fire*, written by Fr. Innocent Montgomery, CFR. The entire work is an investigation into the baptismal call of each Catholic as a means for finding one's true identity in Christ. It contains weekly reflections by different friars who have been led into something called the "desert experience." Each year, Father Innocent brings the new postulants into the Utah desert for several weeks as a way to help them find their identity as rooted in the Father and to bind them together as one unit.

Experiences in the desert range from the somewhat mundane to the absolute extreme of life and death. They live in tents, miles away from any civilization, for weeks. They cannot shower, and they have to find their own way. Many times, they find themselves seeing things from a different perspective for the first time. These powerful moments occur differently for each of them. For one, it may be that he realizes he needs to be more willing to ask for help (and directions). Another may discover he needs to be more willing to trust in those around him rather than feeling as if he has to do everything on his own.

Whatever the case might be, the desert is the place where these young men find something pivotal about themselves because they encounter the Father in a new way. Father Innocent has said that the desert is a privileged place because Jesus went into the desert after his baptism, directly following his election by God to begin his public ministry. In the desert he fasted and prayed and was tempted by the devil. The desert is tough and difficult, but we all need it. If Christ had his time there, then so must we.

The beauty of these desert witnesses of the friars is that they deeply encountered God in both simple and challenging ways. From small and insignificant moments to times when things became very difficult for them as a group, they saw the Lord moving and working. That is the Francis spirit. Simplicity and sacrifice bring about repentance and renewal in the disciples of Christ. Being forced to live in that space for a period of time leads to transformation and peace even though of the road might be bumpy, cold, and tough.

The friars desire true discipleship, and they preach that true friendship with Christ means we actually know Jesus. Seeking to be true disciples means they have deep prayer lives, they serve the poor, they speak about Christ. Living in the desert means they are forced to do this in intimate and radical ways that are both beautiful and purifying. This is exactly why the postulants travel to the desert. It challenges these men who want to enter the order to see if the life of Francis is really for them by giving them a concrete experience of what the Franciscan way does to someone's heart.

The desert, in many ways, is where the journey of a Franciscan begins and ends. Francis understood this, and the CFRs follow his example in their formation process. They recognize that following Jesus is about formation. By this they mean altering one's life to align with the gospel call to holiness. They desire ongoing formation (conversion) in order to become molded more and more into the likeness of Francis and, ultimately, Jesus Christ.

The saint of Assisi offered us the blueprint for how we can take up our cross and go after Christ. The CFRs today carry on that witness, providing us with contemporary examples of living the Franciscan Way. They show us that every single person can align this example to their own lives. Even those of us who are not in religious life can experience conversion and foster revival in the world in the spirit of Saint Francis.

Reflection Questions

- What stands out the most to you about the way the CFRs live? Why does it stand out?
- What are some ways that you can incorporate aspects of their life into your everyday following of Christ?
- What does your prayer life look like? How can it grow and how can it become more intentional?
- Think of someone you know who personifies living radically for God. Why is that way of living attractive to you?

6

The Heart of God
Is the Remedy

God's mercy is greater than even the worst sins of all of humanity combined. Coming to grips with this truth is what enabled Saint Francis to realize that God accepts us despite our brokenness. God is attracted to our dependence on him because, over time, he can use our inadequacies to show us who we really are. Therein lies our identity: We are made for mercy — mercy that renews.

It can be easy to despair over how challenging things are in our Church and world today. Too often we Christians are not truly joyful because being critical and negative is easier than being intentionally grateful for all that God has done. Saint Francis reveals the blueprint for living from joy: Give praise, and be grateful. There is no match for our God. He is great and mighty. He is a guardian and defender. He is King, and he does wonders. When we are rooted in the soil of this truth, we can live and grow from a spirit of true rejoicing.

The work of Saint Francis, to rebuild the Church, is an ongoing mission for each disciple. As we have begun to see, we can only carry out this work through an intense focus on renewing our own life through prayer, reading of the Scriptures, and serving the poor around us while encountering Christ in the relationships nearest to us. Just like Saint Francis, we are invited to renew the earth one stone and one heart at a time. This will be the source of renewal for the wider Church, for our families, and for our communities because it is renewal in the light of Christ's travels to meet people one town and one person at a time.

Jesus invites us to travel with him on our earthly journey, making contact with him each day. We are invited to journey into the life and love of God throughout our lives while always trusting in his goodness because he is who he says he is. This means we must seek to know the heart of God deeply, as Saint Francis did.[1] This is what will bring internal renewal. Since being made like Christ will convert us, and conversion will change the world, we must know *who* we are being made into. We cannot simply learn about God's heart; we must be moved by it.

Discovering the Heart of God

Francis noted, "Whenever you see a poor person, a mirror of the Lord and his poor Mother is placed before you. Likewise in the sick, look closely for the infirmities which He accepted for our sake."[2] If you desire to change your own heart, and you crave renewal in the world, then your heart is prepared to receive God's heart. His love is a gentle mirror that reveals who we are and what we are made for. The remedy for everything resides in that mirror, which is one of poverty and humble obedience.

We need to dig deep and "mine out" just who God is. Once we arrive at a location where we begin to meet him, we will see just how radically he will change how we interact with the world. When we view God from our sinful state, we must always keep in mind that, as the *Catechism of the Catholic Church* mentions, sin is our choice to deaden our trust in the Lord (397). Encountering God's heart allows us to further trust in his goodness above everything else. We will come to realize that his heart is *the* remedy and *the* medicine to heal the wounds of our own heart.

Investigating the heart of God, Father, Son, and Holy Spirit, through a dive into the person of Christ will unveil the answer to the puzzling question of how we can help to change the world through our own individual repentance. Reflecting on Jesus' heart is the best and surest way to look God in the face and see how we are being called to participate in his Trinitarian communion as Francis did.

Christ, quite literally, is the face of God, and when we look at the movements of Jesus' heart on earth, we discover the heart of God. We need to investigate just what made Jesus rejoice, what angered him, what made him sad, and what moved him to be compassionate. If we wish to literally see Christ weep and be brought to joy and be moved to compassion, we must visit the Scriptures. This is where God's face and heart are revealed. Dedicating daily intentional time to praying with the Bible is the best way to meet Jesus this way. These insights will heal us and proclaim to our hearts that we must never get caught up in our own sin, struggles, or darkness. We must look to the prototype for guidance and inspiration. That is what Francis did.

So often we are led to despair because of personal difficulties or because of the crises in the world and the Church. A certain poverty of faith can lead us to distrust rather than repair. And yet, Christ comes to us and asks: "Do you think I do not know what you are going through?" Jesus was God, and he had a huge following during his earthly ministry — but he was ultimately abandoned by those who loved him most and was put to death even though he was the most innocent man ever to live. His physical torture and humiliation are unparalleled in history.

Jesus knows better than anyone else what it is like to suffer.

He knows the movements of our heart and the depths of our joys and sufferings better than anyone ever could. When we meet his heart, he will show us that all he really desires is for us to totally trust him, to believe in him. He will tell us that he sees us, knows us, and loves each of us personally. Knowing him on that level will make us into other Christs and give us the strength to follow him unreservedly, to begin to trust him like Francis did, and to see that renewal is not about charity cases and doing nice deeds. It is about being captivated by Someone.

The friars note that we can see the effect of encountering Christ's heart in the lives of some of his other greatest saints as well. St. Maximilian Kolbe was murdered in Auschwitz after he took the place of a prisoner who had a wife and family. In the heart of Maximilian Kolbe, Jesus snuck into Auschwitz, telling those who were in the darkest place on earth that God stops at nothing to be with us.

St. Damien of Molokai spent his life serving the lepers in Molokai, Hawaii, because no one else was willing to show the heart of Christ to the lepers. Damien later contracted the disease and died serving the least with the greatest love: giving witness to Jesus' heart for those who are left behind by the world or deemed worthless.

St. Leopold of Castelnuovo lived as a Capuchin friar for the majority of his life and spent somewhere between eight and sixteen hours a day hearing confessions. After his death and during World War II, the friary where he spent his life was bombed and left in shambles. One of the only parts of the building left completely untouched was the location of the confessional where Leopold heard thousands of confessions: It still stood as a memorial to the mercy of the heart of the Lord.

In the lives of these three saints one can easily view the heart of God at work. Jesus snuck into Auschwitz, the leper colony, and the confessional, revealing that he wants to get in every dark hole on the earth. These saints also show us that it is in the hidden and simple ways that Christ comes most powerfully to us. Francis found those hidden avenues where God shines, and that is why he was so attracted to those who found themselves on the outskirts.

In the quiet of our own lives, Jesus transmits his will and love for us as well. It is no coincidence that it was in a decrepit chapel, in quiet prayer, that Francis received a calling that would radically transform the Catholic Church and world. This poor man received a culture-altering call in a poor and simple way. God operates in the simple and in the silence. He does so because he refuses to impose himself on us. He will never impose; he will only propose himself.

It is absolutely critical for our own personal conversion that we frequently visit our parish church or churches in our area that are open for prayer. Being alone with Christ in the Eucharist and being quiet regularly will bring about an incredible transformation. We know that Francis "sought out solitary places, making his nightly prayer in lonely and deserted churches."[3] This is a spiritual given. Visiting Christ in his quiet and humble Presence will quite literally change the course of our life.

The Eucharist, the CFRs say, is the most important and greatest example of praying simply as well as the perfect example of how we tend to overlook what is small and hidden. Go and spend time kneeling in a church. Stare at the tabernacle. It is that simple. Hidden in what looks like small pieces of bread, locked up in boxes inside unvisited churches, Jesus' heart is really and truly Present. So let us find him in the small and hidden, and let us make our way to the Eucharist, knowing that his heart saves us from ourselves and makes us holy, like him. Jesus comes to save the brokenhearted and the forgotten, and he himself has accepted brokenness and being overlooked for our sake. If that is not enough to convince us to pray more often and find those who need his love, then I don't know what will.

The Compassion of God

Like Saint Francis, we are also called to turn to the essentials that every saint focuses on: the Gospels, the other, and the Eucharist. When we become experts in the simple things — praying the Bible, praying the Mass, and praying the Rosary — we realize that these supply enough grace for a lifetime if we enter into them wholeheartedly. They are wells that we return to that remain ever new and bring us to a freshness for life that counters our feelings of inadequacy or unworthiness.

Fr. Mark-Mary Ames, CFR, once explained that he had a Scripture professor in seminary who urged his students to pray the Bible by first reading the passage ten times slowly and intentionally. Following the reading, you simply write down questions about the passage. These can be questions on the heart or questions about the details of the passage that strike you. Doing so sounds like a large commitment, but it brings up so much fruit — you will be amazed how the word comes to life!

Investigating specific passages from Jesus' life will allow us to view his heart more profoundly. Making our residence in the word of God will sanctify us. Here, we are going to meditate briefly on the prodigal son (see Lk 15:11–32), the good Samaritan (Lk 10:29–37), and the crowds that moved Jesus with compassion (Mt 9:35–38). These three stories bring us into direct contact with what it means "to suffer with" and be a companion through someone else's passion (this is literally what the word *compassion* means). From his first virtuous encounter with the leper onward, Francis did this, in imitation of Jesus, like no one else — and so must we.

The prodigal son is arguably Jesus' most famous parable. He knew that it would be his most famous, and he could have described God's heart in any fashion he wanted, but he chose a very specific revelation. We can view a beautiful insight into the heart of the Father in the way he "caught sight" of his son while he was still a way off in the distance. Before humanity is even lost, God sends out a search party for our souls.

Here we encounter the heart of God and view exactly what the movement of compassion entails. The father in the story must have spent every day pacing back and forth, peering over the horizon, squinting, wondering: "Will this be the day my son returns? Will I be able to see him today? I wonder if today is the day." True compassion is a constant and deep procession of the heart that never gives up on the one who is suffering.

When the son does return, the father first sees him, then he feels for him, and then he acts toward him (by running to his son). Once he is in front of the son, the father is not interested in the prodigal's explanation for his sins, and he is not concerned with how the son can make it up to him. All he desires is to hold his son and celebrate his return. The father in the story gives us an anointed glimpse into how God looks at the world, and us, in our brokenness and sin. When we are in darkness or find ourselves in a wayward state, the Father is grieving for our loss, and he hurts until we return. Once we return, the only thing God desires is to be with us and love us.

I truly believe that tapping into this truth is what allowed Francis to change so many lives. Francis knew that this is how the Father looked at him in the earlier part of his life. In the midst of his partying, drinking, and rejection of the lepers, the Father waited for him. His sin did not deter the Father from loving him and waiting for him to return. This is probably why Francis never asked for special treatment among the brothers, and why he stressed forgiveness so much. He knew that his conversion was the result of God breaking into his life to rebuild him.

The good Samaritan contains the same movement of compassion found in the prodigal son. The Samaritan sees the hurt and pain in this deserted and beaten man, then he feels it by stopping to engage with the man's suffering, and then he acts by giving aid. Francis and many other spiritual writers have noted that God is attracted, like the Samaritan, to our weakness and brokenness. Like the good Samaritan he is eager to jump into the ditch we find ourselves in so he can bandage us and bring us healing. There is no greater summary of a Saint Francis-like repair mission than these words concerning the good Samaritan. God is moving toward the brokenness of our own hearts and of our times, not away from them.

We are all in need of healing because we have all been robbed of something, like the man in the story. We have been robbed of our original grace by sin. Like the good Samaritan who dives into the ditch and kneels down to peer into the sores of the beaten man, Christ jumps into our human nature and goes to the lowest depths of hell in order to capture what was stolen from us. Our sores do not scare him, and they do not drive him away. The wounds we bear are the very reason for his coming. Conversion is meant to be a beautiful process of intimate restoration.

Finally, we view the compassion of Jesus for the crowds after he calls Matthew, raises Jairus's daughter, and cures several people in need of healing. Christ is making his way into all the towns, healing and teaching, when he sees a large crowd that appears "like sheep without a shepherd" (Mt 9:36). He sees them, feels for them, and then prays that more laborers may go out into the harvest. Here is his cry and prayer that more people will see, feel, and act with compassion toward those who need it the most. Here is the invitation that Francis heard with every fiber of his being.

This preaching and ministering to those in need summarized Francis's life. That is why he barely ever slept: He needed everyone to experience the compassion he felt firsthand. Francis "rarely or never had any rest. ... He filled the whole world with the gospel of Christ; in the course of one day often visiting four or five towns and villages."[4] Here is the challenge that, when answered, leads to new life. Working tirelessly for renewal occurs when we cannot contain the goodness that we have encountered.

We, and so many of our age, too often just meander through our lives, simply going through the motions. We have no one to guide us, and we live shepherdless. This is ultimately why Jesus asked Francis to rebuild his Church: His people were like sheep without a shepherd. We need God's loving and tender care for our heart. We need his compassionate gaze to orient our lives. That is the vision we are called to restore in our own hearts, first and foremost, so that we can direct that same vision in others through our words and witness.

So there we have it: The heart of God is compassion. In these three accounts we can personally see Jesus looking at us, feeling for our circumstances, and acting toward us out of love. Once we are rescued, we are called upon to run out into the harvest and give others the chance to experience the difference that compassion can make in their lives.

The Father relies on us to bring others into closer proximity with him, and he asks us to discern daily where our priorities lie. Saint Augustine once said, "God who created you without you does not justify you without you."[5] God gave us this life out of his abundant love. He does not need us; he wants us, and not just for himself — he desires for us to share his compassionate heart with others in the same spirit in which he gave his blessings to us.

Francis did this naturally because he experienced it profoundly. "In a lonely place, he became wholly absorbed in God, when Jesus Christ appeared to him under the form of a crucifix, at which sight his whole soul seemed to melt away; and so deeply was the memory of Christ's passion pressed on his heart, that it pierced even to the marrow of his bones. From that hour, whenever he thought upon the passion of Christ, he could scarcely restrain his tears and sighs."[6]

After Francis gained a few companions, there was not much on their list of tasks to accomplish other than to sit in the presence of the Lord and be showered with his compassion. They lived in a community, and their focus was rather simple: "They passed their time in continual prayer, and that rather mental than vocal, for they had no ecclesiastical books from which they might chant their canonical hours. But instead of such books they contemplated the Cross of Christ continually, day and night after the example of their father, and being instructed by the discourses which he addressed to them continually concerning the Cross of Christ."[7]

Lasting and transformative faith flows from intimacy with Christ's love and from experiencing the depth of love that is our God. Jesus' reckless love on the cross, through which he forgave his persecutors and never spoke ill of his enemies, shows us how to move forward but also how to be inspired. There is no greater love, no other way to save the world, other than a fixation on this radical action of Jesus Christ, who is the face of compassion.

God's Anger

Did Jesus or Saint Francis ever get angry? If renewal is necessary, that means the current state of affairs is a mess. Does God become enraged by the mess of sin? Can saints get mad at the depravity of human decisions? Finding the answer to these questions is both interesting and important to see how we should respond to evil as well.

Serving the poor means being poor and living like the poor. Francis knew this and acted strongly when his brothers were living in a way that was against the Gospel they were following. One year, while Francis was away, the people of Assisi began to build a house for the friars to stay in, in preparation for a large meeting that was going to take place near St. Mary of the Angels. Upon his return, Francis "climbed up to the roof and started tearing out slates and tiles with a mighty hand. He ordered the brothers also to climb up and to tear down completely that monstrosity against poverty. He said that this would quickly spread throughout the Order, and everyone would take for an example any sign of pretension they saw in that place."[8]

Francis wanted to rip out riches from the lives of the brothers so they could live radically for Christ, tearing through sin and building conversion. In the proper sense of the word, this was anger. St. Thomas Aquinas explains that anger is a response to an evil. One's response to that evil can be good or bad depending on how one goes about responding. A person might experience or witness something wrong. Aquinas uses the word *vengeance* as corresponding to a person's response. Here, vengeance strictly means that one is responding — in justice and charity — to the wrong done. "Wherefore if one desire revenge to be taken in accordance with the order of reason, the desire of anger is praiseworthy, and is called zealous anger."[9]

It justly upset Francis to see that his brothers were not keeping to their commitment — not because he desired to berate them and make them feel bad, but simply because his closeness with Christ revealed that living like Jesus was the way for the human soul to be both healthy and fully alive. That is why he acted in such a way, and that is why God responds to evil and sin with force as well.

Any discussion of God's anger should revolve around Jesus' cleansing of the Temple (see Mt 21:12–17), and how anger reveals God's heart. It is actually the compassion of Jesus that drives him to have the intensity to protect the sanctity of his Father's house (the Temple). By itself, anger is not an evil thing. Anger is a desire for justice. Only when anger leads us to perform an evil action, or allows us to be controlled by rage, does it become evil. A good rule of thumb for anger is this: Does it set you free or bind you in chains? True and righteous anger always brings consolation and freedom.

The context of compassion is crucial to remember. Especially since we know that Jesus always sees, feels, and then acts, like every human. Since Jesus is God, when he sees something wrong, he feels anger, but he always knows how to put it into action perfectly. There is no disconnect between what he sees, what he feels, and how he acts. Again, this was easier for the Lord who, though fully human, was sinless, but something that a restorer also is called to emulate.

Cleansing the Temple was exactly what was needed, because the Lord knows best. Christ saw the evil present and, like removing the tumor of a cancer, he knew it had to go. However, he also knew that the call for repentance and the circumstances for rebuilding need to be followed by something else. What many people often overlook is that, directly after Jesus flips the tables, the next verse refers to him healing the sick and the lame (see Mt 21:14). We can never forget that God's righteous anger is always connected to his loving and healing mercy.

In fact, the act of cleansing would have been incomplete without the acts of healing and forgiveness. Being cleansed means that there is now room for Jesus to work wonders in and through us; he makes space to remind us of who we are and what is most true. Christian baptism does just this, and it also grants each one of us the ability to make room in other people's hearts for the healing work of Christ.

The Christian response to evil and darkness can be contrasted with the anger that so many people and so many Catholics experience in today's world. We can be upset at our age, but we must recall that Christ did not walk around with a consuming bitterness. Jesus did not change the world by being grumpy. His righteous anger in the Temple does not give us license to be angry at the world all the time. The sins of the world and the rejection of his love by the crowds did hurt him, but most often Jesus moved from a position of compassion and mercy, not anger. Anger with an edge is not inspired by the Holy Spirit, and it certainly does not result in fruitful conversions of heart. More often than not, this anger is self-serving and is more concerned with what is going on inside of the person who is angry than the sin they claim they are responding to. Even if a controlling anger is responding to something that is objectively wrong, it is still not productive or spiritually healthy for us.

The cleansing of the Temple reminds us that Jesus' anger was for the sake of communion. We are not speaking about unity as a political catchphrase, but as the driving force behind God's very nature. Jesus desired to place the people in closer proximity with his Father. He was not simply spewing words about how bad everything was. The movement of his heart is the opposite of the devil, who is also known as the accuser. In the same way, our anger must lead us not to accuse, but to bring union as Christ did and as Francis did.

True anger is personified by the realization that, behind this movement, God is fighting for you so he can free you and others from a particular evil. He always comes through with the perfect remedy we need, based on where we are. God's heart does so gently and never intends to shame us in the process. Imitating him, we must never shame others into goodness but allow them to be amazed by the grandeur of truth and love.

In God's eyes, anger and cleansing is always concerned with "giving light and breaking chains," says Fr. Mark-Mary. He will never break us in loving us. The invitation from the heart of God and the heart of Francis is to invite Jesus into your own temple. Ask him to dwell in your heart for the purpose of making more room for his presence. As he makes his way through, plead with him to cleanse you and flip over any sinful tables necessary so that you can make room for the miracles he wants to work in your life. The result will be the experience of a Father's heart and the consequence will be consolation, freedom, and a radical witness to the Gospel.

Let him give light and break chains in your temple. But don't be afraid. His cleansing makes more room for his divine life to rebuild the tables after they are flipped. Then we can rebuild the tables of other people's hearts as well.

Father and Son Moment

In late February 2022, Russia invaded Ukraine. There have been countless political debates about the war and its causes, which are irrelevant here. Social media helped put a human face on the war, in many ways, because of its capacity to spread news over the world in real time.

For example, Ukraine didn't allow men of fighting age to leave the country because they were needed to fight in the war. So many fathers were evacuating their wives and children out of the country. Train stations and bus terminals were overcrowded and became the stage for heart-wrenching scenes. Videos captured the moments when fathers said goodbye to their wives and children, never knowing whether they would see one another again.

One video in particular shook me to the core. A man in his forties embraced his wife, teenage daughter, and young son as a unit as they approached the doors of a bus. Then the dad hugged his wife, and she got on the bus. He gave his daughter a kiss, and she got on the bus. And then, the father picked up his son and hugged him tightly. He placed him on the ground and took a step back with the other dads.

As his young boy went to take his first step onto the bus, the father leaped back toward him and grabbed the top of his head.

He kissed the top of his son's head one last time and held his head against his for a few seconds. Wiping tears from his eyes, he then stepped back away from the bus and waved goodbye from the sidewalk.

He could not help himself. In his mind, this might be (and could very well have been) the last time he would ever see his son. The father needed the son to know that he loved him more than one long goodbye could ever convey. I am sure, if he could have, he would have held him forever.

This type of encounter is deeply biblical and a reflection of the life of God. In the Gospel of Matthew, we see Jesus open his heart and reveal his constant interior disposition toward the Father: "I give praise to you, Father, Lord of heaven and earth, for although you have hidden these things from the wise and the learned you have revealed them to the childlike. Yes, Father, such has been your gracious will" (11:25–27).

So often, Christ brings us to the Father or shows us who he is in word or deed — but in this passage, and in very few other places, Jesus simply says to us, "Look and experience our love." The intimate insights of their infinitely perfect and loving relationship reveal the mystery that always is: Jesus Christ is a son who abundantly delights in being in the presence of his Father. The Lord only desires to look upon the face of the Father (in the Holy Spirit) and see him gaze back into his eyes.

We see deeper revelations of this relationship at Jesus' baptism and his Transfiguration, when we are given access to their love. The heavens open, the Holy Spirit descends, and the Father speaks. On both occasions we hear: "This is my beloved Son, with whom I am well pleased" (Mt 3:17; Mt 17:5). These words are the constant refrain of the Father as he looks upon his Son with deep love. This is also the refrain that so many of us desire to hear from God, and whether we are married, parents, single, or religious, we are asked to participate in the beauty of these words as fathers, mothers, or spiritual fathers and spiritual mothers. The love that is the Trinity is not simply something we observe, but a reality that is meant to transform us.

We are meant to become what we view in Jesus' gaze to the heavens. Jesus gazes into heaven on a few specific occasions in the Gospels. We experience this "look" when Jesus multiplies the loaves and fish for the five thousand (see Mt 14:19); directly before Jesus heals the deaf man (Mk 7:34); when Jesus raises Lazarus from the dead (Jn 11:41); and when Jesus prays to his Father about the hour of his passion arriving (Jn 17:1). Before feeding the five thousand, Jesus looks up to heaven, showing us that he rejoices in feeding us when we are weak and in need. Before healing the deaf man, Jesus looks up to heaven and groans, revealing that he rejoices in healing the broken. Before Jesus raises Lazarus from the dead (the greatest miracle possible), he looks up to heaven because of the joy that comes from destroying death, the very reason he came to earth. Finally, before entering into his suffering, passion, and death, Jesus looks to the Father with an attitude of rejoicing because he will be conquering the powers of evil.

Clearly, the heart of God rejoices during some of the most critical moments in the life of Jesus. These moments show us the refrain of his rejoicing. This is simply what is always happening within their love. Each of us must ask ourselves: Do I live in this gaze? How often am I in that place? The gaze between the Father and the Son is where miracles happen.

We are called to be in that same refrain of rejoicing and of gazing; that place is prayer. As we have seen, at its bedrock prayer is knowing that I am in the presence of another, and I am never alone. That simple but utterly moving knowledge is a call for us to sit in the gaze of the Father toward his Son and of the Son toward his Father. Remaining there allows us to witness what perfect love is, and to participate in that love by simply being present to his presence.

As Catholics, we can see this most beautifully on earth at the sacrifice of the Mass, especially at the moments when the Body of Christ and Blood of Christ are lifted high for all to see. At Mass, we can look up as Jesus looked up to the heavens to pray to his Father. We can literally be placed in the midst of their gaze; we can peer into the beauty of how they look at each other.

Remember that this is a glimpse into the inner life of God and a call by Father, Son, and Spirit for us to live inside their gaze. The joy the three Persons of the Trinity share is beyond all comprehension, and the well of grace that it supplies is infinite. So let us run to the place where heaven and earth meet, and let us sit in prayer with an intentional disposition toward living in the place of their gaze so that we, the converted, can rebuild our world.

The Last Words of Christ

When you are on your deathbed, what will your last testimony be? What do you want your dying words to be? The words that people speak at the end of their lives are critical summaries and exclamation points on their existence. The same holds true for Jesus Christ. Examining what he had to say as he took his last gasps of air can help us better understand what the world needs to hear and feel. These are timeless truths that everyone needs to experience if they are to be transformed.

As Jesus makes his offering of self to the Father, he does so with a heart that is full of us. Traditionally, the Church has described the last words of Christ as being made up of seven different phrases taken from the four Gospels. These are:

1. Father, forgive them, they know not what they do. (Lk 23:34)
2. Amen, I say to you, today you will be with me in Paradise. (Lk 23:43)

3. "Woman, behold your son." Then he said to the disciple, "Behold, your mother." (Jn 19:26–27)
4. My God, My God, why have you forsaken me? (Mt 27:46 and Mk 15:34)
5. I thirst. (Jn 19:28)
6. It is finished. (Mt 27:46 and Mk 15:34)
7. Father, into your hands I commend my spirit. (Lk 23:46)

The first word the Son thinks of and speaks on the cross is "Father." When we boil the life and mission of Christ down to its simplest form, it truly is all about his Father. The cross restores our relationship with God, and the words of Jesus on the cross are deep insights into the perfection of the relationship of the Trinity, as well as pictures of what God wants for his relationship with us.

Historians estimate that the cross would have stood ten feet in the air, so all could see the criminals as the example of what happens when you cross the Romans. From the heights, Jesus makes available the pure form of his relationship with the Father. The mission of Jesus is to become and remain an intimate bridge between humanity and the Father: The cross makes that bridge permanent, and his disciples are meant to fortify and extend that bridge into eternity. This is what we must begin and continue to build in our world.

All of Jesus' last words are some type of representation or example of what it means to be one with the Father. In paradise, the good thief will be with Jesus' father; Saint John will take care of the woman who will sit at the right hand of the Father; the prayer of Psalm 22 (the fourth word) highlights the radical trust of the innocent man who is condemned; Christ's thirst reveals that the Father's heart is always yearning for us; what is finished is Jesus' mission of bringing us back into union with the Father;

and Christ's last words are a complete his offering of all that he is back to his Father.

The chorus of Jesus' last words on the cross echo his first words in the Gospels. When he was twelve years old, he went missing on a visit to Jerusalem, and his mother and father found him in the Temple with the teachers. They asked their son why he went missing like this. His answer: "Why were you looking for me? Did you not know that I must be in my Father's house?" (Lk 2:49). Jesus will always be in the midst of accomplishing his Father's business.

This sounds extremely simple. However, the simple things are what we need the most, and they are what we often overlook. The simple things are the beautiful things that are good for us to contemplate simply because they are good in and of themselves. The heart of God as shown in the relationship between the Father and the Son is simply beautiful and worth our attention. Christ was always about the business of his Father. Are we?

Are we more concerned with what we want to do, over and above what others need and what God might be asking us to do? Today, we are being asked to consider the last words of Jesus and contemplate them slowly and deeply, because life is too often very difficult and challenging. In hardship and pain, we will be tempted to think that the Father is not with us or that we are all alone.

We might also be tempted to doubt the goodness of God because of poor examples of motherhood or fatherhood in our own lives. Whatever our experience was, we should rest in the consolation that our Father stops at nothing to be with us. Saint Francis, in fact, had a very tough relationship with his own father. His dad even went so far as to chain him up in the house to prevent his missionary zeal.

In the famous call of Francis by God we can see the heart of God redeeming Francis's poor experiences with his own father. The rebuilding of the Church came inevitably along with the restoration of his relationship with the Father. So even in the suffering and pain, we are asked to make it all about the Father's business. Jesus' heart on the cross is exclaiming to the world that, in our suffering, he wants us to be in his presence. Above all, this is what he communicates to us about his heart during his time on the cross and in his last words on earth.

Allow the mysteries of Calvary to console you. Sit in the fact that you are restored anew in the perfect offering of the Son to the Father, that your own personal restoration is needed to carry out the rebuilding work that Jesus started and that Francis continued.

Faith Appears Lifeless

Following the reality of Calvary, we are asked to rest in the silence and, yes, the darkness of what comes on Good Friday. Right now, the world and the Church seem to be very much in the heart of our own Good Friday afternoon. Not to be dramatic, but if you spend too much time viewing the bad news, it can seem as if Jesus' dead body is still hanging on the cross.

It appears as if evil and death have won because Christ has taken his last breath and is in the process of being taken down from the cross. The most powerful person to ever live lies lifeless in the arms of his mother. All of the true but devastating facts about the impact of faith in our world can also appear overwhelming and final. It is as if we have closed the tomb on our savior, and we are keeping vigil over his destruction.

Francis and the friars would often travel from city to city and preach to the people. Francis would always ask the local bishop for permission. As his name spread, it seemed that no bishop refused him except the Bishop of Imola (near Bologna). He told Francis that it was his role to preach, not the friars'. Englebert recounts what happened next:

With a courteous bow, Francis withdrew — but he was
back an hour later. "Are you back again?" boomed the
bishop. "What do you want now?" "Your Excellency," replied Francis, "when a father drives his son out the door,
there is nothing left for him to do but to come back in
through the window. So I, as your loving son, have not
hesitated to come back to see you."[10]

The bishop then gave way to Francis's request. "The time to
ridicule and insult was over. From now on the Little Poor Man
stole all men's hearts through his persistence and dedication to
proclaiming Christ. Instead of sowing — like so many of the re-
formers — the seeds of rebellion and hatred, he built up, showed
the tasks that needed to be done, and nourished souls eager for
perfection and holiness."

When it looks like we have lost and things will not be restored in our time, we must persevere and march toward the
empty tomb with perseverance, vigor, and deep faith. The disciples on that first Holy Triduum weekend were also not expect-
ing anything else to happen regarding their teacher's life and
mission. The show was over for them, and they were worried
that what happened to Jesus might happen to them next. At the
moment of salvation, they fled, and in the aftermath they lived
in fear. Modern followers of Christ are called not to make the
same mistake.

It looks like our world, and in many ways our Church, are
dead and buried. The rock is in front of their tomb, and it's over.
The reality is that the tomb is deep and dark — but it is empty. Our world and Church are not defeated, they are simply in
need of being resurrected. Christ wants our aid in bringing this
about, so he sends great saints to teach us the path forward. Let
us employ the way of Francis because it is true to the Gospel and
because it is interconnected with the reality and mission of the

Resurrection.

In his encyclical *Rite Expiatis,* Pope Pius XI wrote, "It seems necessary for us to affirm that there has never been anyone in whom the image of Jesus Christ and the evangelical manner of life shone forth more lifelike and strikingly than in St. Francis ... appearing to his contemporaries and to future generations almost as if he were the Risen Christ."

Restoration will come. Our nation, globe, and Church will be rebuilt and restored. The Resurrection will win. In the meantime, and to accomplish that, let us be like Saint Francis. Let us be renewed within by the power and love of Christ so that we can appear to others as mirrors of Jesus. Strive to walk in his footsteps, because it is individual conversion that will truly change the world.

So be converted — and let us begin!

Reflection Questions

- Focusing on how there needs to be large-scale change is often easier than reflecting on the very next step we need to take in our lives. What is something you can do tomorrow, this week, and this month to bring about deeper conversion in your own life and those around you?
- What is it about God's heart that stands out to you the most from the words of the friars, and the Franciscan lens of viewing Christ?
- How can the last words of Christ strengthen a commitment of yours to pray or love those around you?
- What appears most lifeless to you (the Church, your parish, the country, your family, your prayer life, etc.)? How can Francis's wisdom shine a light on the truth of the resurrection in this aspect of your heart?

Afterword

To salvage the doors is difficult. It takes attentiveness and commitment.

Speaking about renewal is rather easy; faithfully responding to the invitation is the real challenge. The first step for Francis and his friars in changing the world was to implement habits that bring about deeper personal conversion, and this must be our response as well. We can never receive enough restoration to our soul on this side of heaven, so we embark on the journey together, with our eyes fixed on Christ.

This book highlighted the reality that we face many problems in our communities, parishes, dioceses, in the worldwide Church, and in our country. The intention behind highlighting our shortcomings is not to deplore how horrid our contemporary world might be or place blame for the problems. Pessimism is not the motive either. Rebuilding anything in life, physical or immaterial, requires that we strip away the paint and tear down walls. If the way we have been living, evangelizing, and governing is not working, then we must change. Yet even while we must let go of the dysfunctions, there is so much to salvage — like the Scriptures, the sacraments, and those people who live and breathe evangelization. These gems are absolutely essential and indispensable. But a construction site is noisy, dirty, and chaotic, and in order to arrive at the place the Church needs to be, we must radically reimagine how we do ministry, catechesis, and formation in the Church.

That can only happen if individual hearts first begin to fall in love with Christ.

Falling in love with Christ causes friction, and many will look to other, easier paths. This is, however, our only option; it does not require a new Gospel or another Messiah. A repair mission in the spirit of Francis is about returning to what has always been true and what has always been right in front of our faces, but has been lost due to lack of intentional discipleship and apostolic fervor. This is not an accusation, but rather a challenge to all contemporary men and women of faith.

We must find a construction site in need of renewal, like Saint Francis did. After he first heard his call from God at San Damiano to "rebuild my church," Francis sold his horse and items from his father's merchant shop. His father became quite upset, rightfully so, and brought Francis before the bishop. Francis's mission was just, but the way he went about it was suspect for those of his time.

The bishop ordered that Francis repay his father for what was taken from the shop. So he took off his fine clothing and placed all the money he had on top of the pile of his fancy garb. Then he went off into the snow with only a hairshirt on, singing as he made his way toward San Damiano, and began repairing its stone walls and those of nearby St. Peter's and St. Mary of the Angels at the Portiuncula. While God was asking him to do more than simply repair buildings with stones, Francis first needed a place, along with his followers, to pray. Not simply because without prayer we can do nothing, but also for one obvious reason that we often neglect to acknowledge: Francis was radically in love with Jesus Christ. He had to have places where he could spend time with God and be in his presence because Christ was the love of Francis's life. That was the reason why Francis was becoming a new fool for Christ: He simply needed to be with him as much as possible.

Our construction site model must begin the same way. We must be people of immense and radical prayer. Again, not just because we need it for strength, but because we have fallen outlandishly in love with God. If we do not have a physical place or location on our daily schedule for prayer, then we need to build one. Make a move to find that best physical spot and that most suitable location on your schedule, one day at a time — just like Francis picked up one stone at a time.

Start with yourself. Commit to prayer and make it about intimacy. Promise to give God access to your heart and give him significant space in your daily calendar, not just the throw-away minutes at the end of a day. In the same vein, name the sins that are most in control of you. Maybe it is gossip, a lack of trust, lust, or anger. Whatever you find that most separates you from God, root it out by a reliance on the Sacrament of Reconciliation and a radical dependence on God to heal you.

Then we can move on to having that radically loving relationship with God that will inspire us to love and act for others in a dynamic way. There is no other option for the disciple. The twelve apostles left everything because they knew that their relationship with Jesus needed to be everything. They saw the way the Lord looked into their hearts, and they knew that love could be found nowhere else. Only once they lived and moved and had their being from that starting point could they go out and carry Jesus' mission to renew the face of the earth.

From this place of secure attachment to God, focus on your

immediate neighbors. For whom am I being called to sacrifice in a unique way, right now? A spouse, a child, a parent, or a co-worker might be first on the list; serve them as if they were Jesus himself. Give them attention and love as if they were the only person in the world. That is how Francis changed lives, and it is how you will begin to renew the lives of others.

Like Francis, always be on the lookout for a construction site that needs repairing. It could be broken relationships in your family, or maybe a person you know struggling with addiction. Perhaps you need to forgive or be forgiven by a loved one or long-lost friend. Whatever that first stone must be, we must begin somewhere — so let us pick up that stone. Doing so will lead us out on an epic journey filled with the love of Christ who is our goal and our everything. He will repair our hearts, our lives, and our world; we just have to give him permission.

Saint Francis, pray for us.

Acknowledgments

This book is the result of a deep encounter with the life, words, and message of St. Francis of Assisi. This occurred, first and foremost, because of my own human weakness and the love of my wife, Joanna. Her witness and simple following of Christ continue to be the cause of tremendous growth in my ongoing conversion as well as in my role as a husband and father.

Gaining access to the details of the life and words of Saint Francis was primarily possible because of the guidance of Fr. Mark-Mary Ames, CFR. His friendship, faith, and support made this work possible. While he could never school me on the basketball court, he has continued to school me in what it means to follow in the footprints of Francis and Christ.

I also need to thank the other members of the *Poco a Poco* podcast, whom I have been blessed to get to know in small ways: Fr. Pierre-Toussaint, Fr. Innocent Montgomery, and Fr. Angelus Montgomery. The mission and shared faith of their platform and community allowed for a deepening of my understanding and appreciation for Franciscan spirituality. For that, I am forever grateful.

My cousin, Stephen Deere, was also a critical reviewer in the early brainstorm stages of this process. His insights and comments were very helpful in shaping what the final product of this book would become. His friendship and faith is something I am truly grateful for.

Finally, I would like to thank Rebecca Martin, Mary Beth Giltner, and the entire OSV staff who have been invaluable in this process. Their insight and patience with me allowed for this work to arrive at a place where it can, hopefully, bring about new life in people's hearts and in the Church.

Notes

Chapter 1: Francis and His Life's Work

1. Kajetan Esser, OFM, *The Writings of St. Francis of Assisi* (A Publication of the Franciscan Archive, 1999), 5.

2. Esser, *The Writings of St. Francis of Assisi*, 8.

3. Omer Englebert, *St. Francis of Assisi: A Biography* (Cincinnati, OH: Servant Books, 2013), 33.

4. Ibid., 70.

5. Ibid.

6. Saint Bonaventure, *The Life of St. Francis of Assisi: A Biography of St. Francis of Assisi and Stories of His Followers* (Charlotte, NC: TAN Books, 2010), 15.

7. Ibid., 5.

8. Esser, *The Writings of St. Francis of Assisi*, 20–21.

9. Ibid., 33.

10. Ibid., 34.

11. Saint Bonaventure, *The Life of St. Francis of Assisi*, 74.

12. Ibid., 15–16.

13. Ibid., 21–22.

14. Esser, *The Writings of St. Francis of Assisi*, 26.

15. Bonaventure, *The Life of St. Francis of Assisi*, 22.

16. *Catechism of the Catholic Church*, 2448.

17. Bonaventure, *The Life of St. Francis of Assisi*, 33.

18. Ibid., 13.

19. Ibid., 15.

20. Esser, *The Writings of St. Francis of Assisi*, 41.

21. Ibid., 50.

Chapter 2: The Francis Way

1. Esser, *The Writings of St. Francis of Assisi*, 5.

2. Bonaventure, *The Life of St. Francis of Assisi*, 4.

3. Esser, *The Writings of St. Francis of Assisi*, 7.

4. Ibid.

5. Ibid.

6. Ibid.

7. Ibid.

8. Ibid.

9. Ibid., 8.

10. Ibid.

11. Ibid., 12.

12. Ibid., 42.

13. Ibid., 47.

14. Ibid.

15. Ibid., 49.

16. Ibid., 80.

17. Ibid., 105.

18. Benedict Groeschel, CFR, *The Reform of Renewal* (San Francisco: Ignatius Press, 1990), 144.

19. Englebert, *St. Francis of Assisi*, 199.

20. Erasmo Leiva-Merikakis, *Fire of Mercy, Heart of the Word: Meditations on the Gospel according to Saint Matthew* (San Francisco: Ignatius Press, 1996–2021), 70.

21. Regis J. Armstrong, OFM, Cap., et al, eds., *Francis of Assisi: Early Documents, Vol. II The Founder* (St. Bonaventure, NY: Franciscan Institute of St. Bonaventure University), 83.

22. Groeschel, *The Reform of Renewal*, 16.

23. *The Writings of Francis of Assisi* in *Vol. I The Saint* (St. Bonaventure, NY: Franciscan Institute of St. Bonaventure University), 64–65.

24. Groeschel, *The Reform of Renewal*, 20

25. Ibid., 194.

26. Ibid., 198.

27. Englebert, *St. Francis of Assisi*, 273.

28. Groeschel, *The Reform of Renewal*, 22.

29. Ibid., 36.

30. Ibid., 46 (emphasis added).

31. Ibid., 160.

32. Ibid., 47.

Chapter 3: Beginning the Process of Rebuilding

1. Eric Wargo, "How Many Seconds to a First Impression?" *The Association for Psychological Science Observer* (July 1, 2006), https://www.psychologicalscience.org/observer/how-many-seconds-to-a-first-impression.

2. Joseph Langford, *Mother Teresa's Secret Fire* (Huntington, IN: Our Sunday Visitor, 2008), 54.

3. Julian Speyer, *The Life of Saint Francis*, in Regis J. Armstrong, OFM, Cap., et al, eds., *Francis of Assisi: Early Documents, Vol. I The Saint* (St. Bonaventure, NY: Franciscan Institute of St. Bonaventure University), 379.

4. Thomas of Celano, *The Desire of a Soul*, in Regis J. Armstrong, OFM, Cap., et al, eds., *Francis of Assisi: Early Documents, Vol. II The Founder* (St. Bonaventure, NY: Franciscan Institute of St. Bonaventure University), 343.

5. Ibid., 401.

6. Ibid.

Chapter 4: Pillars of Change

1. Bonaventure, *The Life of St. Francis of Assisi*, 73.

2. As quoted in Thomas of Celano, *The Desire of a Soul.*

3. Thomas of Celano, *The Desire of a Soul*, 315.

4. Mark-Mary Ames, CFR, *Habits for Holiness: Small Steps for Making Big Spiritual Progress* (West Chester, PA: Ascension Press, 2021), 5.

5. Ames, *Habits for Holiness*, 20.

6. Ibid., 21.

7. Ibid.

Chapter 5: Franciscan Friars of the Renewal

1. Ames, *Habits for Holiness*, 1.

2. Englebert, *St. Francis of Assisi*, 117.

3. Bonaventure, *The Life of St. Francis of Assisi*, 46.

4. G. K. Chesterton, *Saint Thomas Aquinas and Saint Francis of Assisi* (San Francisco: Ignatius Press, 2002), 246.

5. Thomas of Celano, *The Desire of a Soul,* 334.

6. Ibid., 263.

7. Ibid., 342–343.

8. Pius XI, *Rite Expiatis*, vatican.va.

Chapter 6: The Heart of God Is the Remedy

1. Many of the spiritual insights contained in this chapter came from the CFRs' *Poco a Poco* weekly podcast. In the podcast, the friars discuss the importance of prayer, virtue, and intimacy with Jesus Christ. The friars have described the podcast as "a source of rest, encouragement, refreshment, and renewal for all pilgrims, helping them to discern and make the next best step. *Poco a Poco*, little by little, step by step, we're making our pilgrimage to the Father's house."

2. Thomas of Celano, *The Desire of a Soul*, 303.

3. Bonaventure, *The Life of St. Francis of Assisi*, 82.

4. Thomas of Celano, *The Life of Saint Francis of Assisi* in Regis J. Armstrong, OFM, Cap., et al, eds., *Francis of Assisi: Early Docu-*

ments, *Vol. I The Saint* (St. Bonaventure, NY: Franciscan Institute of St. Bonaventure University), 266.

5. Augustine, *Sermo* 169, 11, 13 (PL 38:923).

6. Bonaventure, *The Life of St. Francis of Assisi*, 5.

7. Ibid., 24.

8. Thomas of Celano, *The Desire of a Soul*, 285.

9. Thomas Aquinas, *Summa Theologiae* II-II. q. 158. A. 2.

10. Englebert, *St. Francis of Assisi*.

About the Author

Thomas Griffin lives on Long Island with his wife and two sons. He holds a master's degree in theology and is currently a master's candidate in philosophy. He is the chairperson of the religion department at a Catholic high school where he teaches apologetics and works in campus ministry. He is the director of evangelization at his parish, St. Rose of Lima. Thomas is the founder and editor-in-chief of a nonprofit evangelization company called the Empty Tomb Project, which publishes online articles and a print magazine six times a year. He writes regularly for several online magazines, including *Busted Halo*, *Crisis* magazine, SpiritualDirection.com, *The Federalist*, and Word on Fire.

You might also like:

Saint Francis of Assisi Story Cards
By Franciscan Friars of the Renewal and Greenhouse Collective

Children will be delighted with this beautiful set of cards that, when placed together, form a large illustration of Saint Francis' life. Each flashcard-sized piece features an event in the great saint's life, while the reverse side tells a story and includes questions, Scripture, and an activity to help children learn to love Jesus like Saint Francis did.